ADJUSTMENT AND EQUITY IN DEVELOPING COUNTRIES

GENERAL EDITOR
Christian Morrisson

ADJUSTMENT AND EQUITY IN DEVELOPING COUNTRIES

A NEW APPROACH

By

François Bourguignon and Christian Morrisson

DEVELOPMENT CENTRE
OF THE ORGANISATION FOR ECONOMIC CO-OPERATION AND DEVELOPMENT

ORGANISATION FOR ECONOMIC CO-OPERATION AND DEVELOPMENT

Pursuant to Article 1 of the Convention signed in Paris on 14th December 1960, and which came into force on 30th September 1961, the Organisation for Economic Co-operation and Development (OECD) shall promote policies designed:

— to achieve the highest sustainable economic growth and employment and a rising standard of living in Member countries, while maintaining financial stability, and thus to contribute to the development of the world economy;

— to contribute to sound economic expansion in Member as well as non-member countries in the process of economic development; and

— to contribute to the expansion of world trade on a multilateral, non-discriminatory basis in accordance with international obligations.

The original Member countries of the OECD are Austria, Belgium, Canada, Denmark, France, Germany, Greece, Iceland, Ireland, Italy, Luxembourg, the Netherlands, Norway, Portugal, Spain, Sweden, Switzerland, Turkey, the United Kingdom and the United States. The following countries became Members subsequently through accession at the dates indicated hereafter: Japan (28th April 1964), Finland (28th January 1969), Australia (7th June 1971) and New Zealand (29th May 1973). The Commission of the European Communities takes part in the work of the OECD (Article 13 of the OECD Convention). Yugoslavia has a special status at OECD (agreement of 28th October 1961).

The Development Centre of the Organisation for Economic Co-operation and Development was established by decision of the OECD Council on 23rd October 1962.

The purpose of the Centre is to bring together the knowledge and experience available in Member countries of both economic development and the formulation and execution of general economic policies; to adapt such knowledge and experience to the actual needs of countries or regions in the process of development and to put the results at the disposal of the countries by appropriate means.

The Centre has a special and autonomous position within the OECD which enables it to enjoy scientific independence in the execution of its task. Nevertheless, the Centre can draw upon the experience and knowledge available in the OECD in the development field.

*   *   *

Publié en français sous le titre :

AJUSTEMENT ET ÉQUITÉ
DANS LES PAYS EN DÉVELOPPEMENT
UNE APPROCHE NOUVELLE

*   *   *

Foreword

This work is one of a series produced under the Development Centre's programme on "Structural Adjustment and Equitable Growth". Following approval by the Centre's Advisory Board, a macro-micro model was developed and refined. This was published as a Development Centre Technical Paper (No. 1) in 1989. The model was then modified and applied to a number of developing countries and the results are being collected in this series. This volume provides a synthesis of the seven country studies and makes recommendations for equitable adjustment policies.

SPECIAL OFFER

For the purchase of eight books to be published in the "Adjustment and Equity in Developing Countries" Series (Ecuador, Chile, Ivory Coast, Ghana, Indonesia, Malaysia, Morocco and synthesis volume):
(41 91 00 1) FF835 £110.00 US$198.00 DM320

ALSO AVAILABLE

Adjustment and Equity in Chile *by Patricio Meller* (1992)
(41 91 16 2) ISBN 92-64-23619-3 FF130 £17.00 US$31.00 DM50

Adjustment and Equity in Ecuador *by Alain de Janvry, Elisabeth Sadoulet, André Fargeix* (1991)
(41 91 15 1) ISBN 92-64-13539-1 FF130 £17.00 US$31.00 DM50

Adjustment and Equity in Indonesia *by Erik Thorbecke, with the collaboration of Roger Downey, Steven Keuning, Byung Kim, David Roland-Holst, David Berrian and the Centre for World Food Studies* (1992)
(41 91 19 1) ISBN 92-64-13651-7 FF130 £17.00 US$31.00 DM50

Adjustment and Equity in Malaysia *by David Demery, Lionel Demery* (1992)
(41 91 20 1) ISBN 92-64-13601-0 FF130 £17.00 US$31.00 DM50

Adjustment and Equity in Morocco *by Christian Morrisson* (1991)
(41 91 21 1) ISBN 92-64-13589-8 FF130 £17.00 US$31.00 DM50

Development Centre Seminars

Strategic Options for Latin America in the 1990s *edited by Colin I. Bradford Jr.* (1992)
(41 92 04 1) ISBN 92-64-13634-7 FF175 £22.00 US$42.00 DM68

Development Centre Studies

External Trade and Income Distribution *by François Bourguignon, Christian Morrisson* (1989)
(41 89 03 1) ISBN 92-64-13250-3 FF190 £23.00 US$40.00 DM78

Strategic Industries in a Global Economy: Policy issues for the 1990s (1991)
(03 91 03 1) ISBN 92-64-13559-6 FF120 £12.00 US$20.00 DM35

Prices charged at the OECD Bookshop.
THE OECD CATALOGUE OF PUBLICATIONS and supplements will be sent free of charge
on request addressed either to OECD Publications Service,
or to the OECD Distributor in your country.

Table of Contents

List of Tables and Figures

Acknowledgements

We would like to express our gratitude to the Swedish International Development Agency for the financial support which permitted this project to be carried out. The authors also thank Stephan Haggard for his observations and their Development Centre colleagues, Jean Bonvin and Colm Foy, who kindly reread the manuscript.

Preface

In 1987, the Development Centre initiated a research project on "Adjustment Programmes and Equitable Growth". There was a pressing need for such a study because of the adverse effects of adjustment programmes on employment, wages and government spending for education and health. Unfortunately, the issue remains no less important today, for in a number of countries adjustment programmes hit low-income families particularly hard and at times give rise to violent protests, however valid the reasons are for re-establishing macroeconomic equilibrium.

Under this project, the Development Centre carried out seven studies, devoted to Chile, Côte d'Ivoire, Ecuador, Ghana, Indonesia, Malaysia and Morocco, which have been or are about to be published. This sample of countries is highly varied, whether considered from a geographic, historical or demographic standpoint. Furthermore, some of these countries instituted adjustment measures in co-operation with the IMF following a financial crisis, while others independently carried out adjustment policies before or long after a crisis. Consequently, the lessons we can draw from these studies have a broader applicability than that of a single case study. This is all the more desirable since there are different regional experiences: the performances of South-East Asia and Latin America are quite unequal.

Thus we considered it indispensable to have a synthesis of these studies as the culmination of this large project, on which some 20 researchers have worked. This synthesis was undertaken by F. Bourguignon and C. Morrisson, who have striven for clarity of presentation and avoided technicalities in order to make the results accessible to all readers. At the end of such a research programme, it is evident that those responsible for making economic policy expect some practical answers to their problems; thus the authors have devoted a long chapter to practical conclusions and recommendations for these policy makers. Chapter V, which takes political factors into account, dispels the dangerous illusions of avoiding adjustment, reveals the advantages of an early adjustment and leads us to rethink stabilization programmes. Since stabilization measures are not neutral, a given reduction of external deficit could be obtained with measures having different social costs, and since each country has a specific situation, standard programmes should not used; rather governments should design programmes according to their needs, using a model to estimate the effects of alternative policies and to adapt these measures to the country's characteristics. Even if the adjustment with the least social cost is chosen, however, it is not possible to avoid an increase of poverty among certain groups and because of disequilibria, notably budgetary, these countries are not able to finance compensatory transfers. Only donors can resolve this problem, by being associated with the adjustment policy as a whole.

The earlier chapters summarise the case studies and their methodology. Chapters I to III discuss the origins of adjustment and the evolution of unemployment, incomes, government transfers and poverty during the adjustment period. This picture reveals a different history for each country and shows that these developments are due either to the adjustment and the crisis which preceded it, or to long-term trends. This complexity makes it indispensable to use a model for estimating the effects of each stabilization measure. Chapter IV is devoted to a non-technical presentation of the model and to analysis of the social effects of these measures, such as they appeared in the five countries for which several stabilization policies have been simulated with a model.

We are indebted to F. Bourguignon and C. Morrisson for a work that, though short, is essential for economic policy makers and academics, as it is a milestone in the study of the social consequences of adjustment and proposes new instruments for the preparation of adjustment programmes. In the process, the Development Centre participated at just the right moment in the indispensable collective effort of formulating programmes that reconcile stabilization with the struggle against inequalities and poverty.

Louis Emmerij
President of the OECD Development Centre
March 1992

Executive Summary

Genesis of the Crisis and Adjustment

The crisis at the beginning of the 1980s resulted from external shocks experienced by economies that had become more or less fragile. In fact, during the 1970s many countries became increasingly indebted because they used foreign loans to finance a growing proportion of their investments, which sometimes proved not very productive. As a result, their current accounts went into deficit and they had to borrow more and more to pay interest on debts and continue to invest. In some cases, the external disequilibrium coincided with a budget deficit and/or inflation. The situation was fairly healthy in only two countries of our sample: Malaysia, because it had few debts, and Indonesia, because petroleum enabled it to repay a large debt.

Two external shocks struck the countries studied at the beginning of the 1980s: a rise in interest rates accompanied by a scarcity of international credit, and a deterioration of the terms of trade. As a result, these already fragile economies experienced financial crises and had to institute stabilization programmes in co-operation with the IMF, the *sine qua non* for obtaining new loans. This classic example of adjustment to a crisis is illustrated by four countries: Chile, Côte d'Ivoire, Ecuador and Morocco. In contrast, Indonesia and Malaysia adjusted before the crisis without having to go to the IMF. Ghana, having rejected adjustment and remained in a state of crisis for ten years, had to reduce its imports to the low level of its exports since it could not borrow. Thus apart from the classic case, adjustment can occur either before or after a crisis.

To avoid any confusion, the term **stabilization** will be reserved for measures concerning demand and **structural adjustment,** for policies concerning supply. Stabilization programmes deal directly with the financial crisis, reducing demand to decrease the exterior deficit. The programmes always involve similar measures: cutting public investments, reducing or stabilizing current expenditure (including wages), slowing the growth of the money supply and devaluing the currency. Although we observed these measures in all the countries studied, the severity of a given measure depended on the case. Thus the fall in investment was much greater in Côte d'Ivoire and Morocco than in the two Asian countries, which undertook programmes that on the whole were much less harsh because their economies were in trouble but not in crisis.

Structural adjustment programmes, though involving quite different measures from country to country, are based on a common principle: the need for a liberalisation of both foreign and domestic trade to increase the economy's efficiency. Privatisation measures are derived from this principle, since privatisation is not an end in itself; rather, the goal is to ensure — either by privatisation or by management reform — that state enterprises respect the laws of the market like other enterprises. Domestic liberalisation leads to agricultural price rises and abolition of the monopolies which sell to or buy from farmers. The most important measure, however, is the lowering of customs tariffs because this entails a restructuring of the whole economy, especially of industry.

Employment, Incomes and Poverty during Adjustment

Employment trends differ in urban and rural areas. The situation generally does not deteriorate in the latter, for the labour supply grows more slowly in rural areas than in cities, while adjustment is to some extent favourable to agriculture as a result of devaluation, rises in producer prices and trade liberalisation. On the other hand, in cities the braking of demand slows growth in the modern sector whereas the labour supply grows rapidly (4 to 5 per cent a year). This has two consequences: a sudden rise in unemployment and a swelling of the informal sector, which serves as a refuge in countries without unemployment benefits (except in Chile).

As its active population grows, the informal sector produces more, but since demand is stagnant or declining the adjustment is made through lower prices, and therefore lower incomes of those working in the informal sector. Wage trends in the modern sector depend on the country. In the classic case of an adjustment during a crisis, real wages decline in the public and private sectors. On the other hand, in the countries which adjusted before a crisis, and therefore made only moderate budget cuts, this decline did not occur. Furthermore, wages rose in Ghana where they had been falling since the 1970s. The movement of profits seemed more favourable, the division between wages and profits evolving in favour of profits, but the adjustment period is very discriminating: some enterprises suffer losses or go bankrupt during adjustment as a result of the cuts in public construction expenditure or liberalisation of trade.

Trends in agricultural incomes and employment were favourable during adjustment. In none of the countries was a fall in income observed, except for small peasants in Ecuador who, lacking land, derive part of their income from work in the non-agricultural sector and suffered from the recession in this sector.

Apparently, adjustment widely affected public transfers or services: some food subsidies were reduced, while per capita expenditure on education and health declined. But there can be exceptions, for these expenditures increased in Malaysia. In the countries where they declined, the government had sharply cut wages of public employees so that although per capita expenditure fell, the services continued to increase: in Morocco school enrolments increased, depending on the level of instruction, by 10 to 29 per cent, despite a per capita fall in expenditure of 11 per cent. Moreover, the abolition of some subsidies was often accompanied by compensatory measures in favour of the poor (for example, Ghana's Programme of Actions to Mitigate the Social Costs of Adjustment), so there was an overall fall in transfers only in Côte d'Ivoire.

In these conditions, family living standards do not necessarily fall during adjustment. There were improvements in Indonesia, Malaysia and rural areas of Ghana and Morocco. On the other hand, there was a deterioration in Ecuador, Chile (except for the richest and poorest) and urban areas of Morocco and especially Côte d'Ivoire.

Consequently, during adjustment poverty declined in the two Asian countries, in rural areas of Morocco, where a majority of the poor live, and in Ghana. In Côte d'Ivoire, poverty remained stable in the north and east, where it predominates, but it increased in urban areas. Finally, there were increases in poverty in Chile and Ecuador. These results are related to the timing of adjustment: the best way to ensure that the poor do not suffer from adjustment is to adjust before a crisis. Government decisions also influence the results: some governments provided for compensatory transfers to the poor, while others either made no provision at all (for example, Ecuador) or allowed transfers only to the very poorest (as in Chile).

The Usefulness of Modelling

Can the preceding description of the crisis, adjustment and its apparent consequences on poverty, however precise and detailed, serve as a basis for definite conclusions about the effects of the economic policies in the countries of the sample, or further, about measures implemented in one country but not another, or even about completely new policies? Obviously, that cannot be done with a historical analysis alone.

This project's methodology consisted of carrying out a series of experiments on "scalemodels", theoretical models of the economies considered. The construction of such models in itself was a major undertaking since their degree of detail had to permit evaluation of adjustment policies. Thus it was necessary that they allow us to study the impact of a set of adjustment measures not only on large economic aggregates but on various socio-economic groups in the population.

Of the seven countries in the sample, five were completely modeled, and most often the models serve as the basis for the conclusions concerning the efficacy, inefficacy, or effects on income distribution of one or another adjustment measure. These models should also permit us to correct for the economic magnitudes of components which are not attributable to adjustment policies and, in contrast with a purely historical analysis, to determine the effects of the adjustment policies alone.

Although different on several counts, the models used for Côte d'Ivoire, Ecuador, Indonesia, Malaysia and Morocco were constructed on a common principle: more or less detailed microeconomic modelling of the sectoral structure of production and prices and the socio-economic structure of incomes, linked with a macroeconomic model capable of representing and analysing the effects of the main components of the stabilization and structural adjustment policies. The microeconomic modelling is in large part directly inspired by calculable general equilibrium (CGE) models, while the macroeconomic modelling entailed introducing into the preceding models a whole set of alternative "closures" to represent equilibrium, or often disequilibria, of large aggregated markets for goods, services, labour, money, foreign currency and various other physical or financial assets.

The models are used to study in detail:

a. cutting public expenditures;

b. monetary contraction;

c. devaluation of the exchange rate; and

d. certain structural measures involving the domestic taxation system (indirect taxes) and customs duties.

For some countries, the total cost of several adjustment policies, including the policy actually used, was also compared with a scenario of not adjusting.

The Illusion of Not Adjusting and Advantages of an Anticipated Adjustment

If non-adjustment is defined as a government's refusal to modify its budgetary, monetary or exchange policies — a refusal that compels it, once the possibilities for borrowing abroad have been exhausted, to resort to rationing, beginning with imports — then all adjustment policies are, according to our simulations, more efficient (less fall in economic activity) and more equitable (smaller increases in poverty) than not adjusting.

The history of Ghana confirms these results. The rejection of adjustment by this country at the beginning of the 1970s has had enormous costs: fall of per capita income, output of commercial crops, exports and imports; a large decline in wages and in agricultural incomes, which led to a disastrous increase in poverty. Consequently, there is a need to refocus political debates about adjustment, which are misleading because comparisons of adjustment and non-adjustment count the costs of adjustment (often confused with the costs of the crisis) but do not take into account the costs of not adjusting.

On the other hand, the only way to avoid the costs of adjustment in crisis is to adjust before a crisis. As the disequilibria are less severe at that time, a smaller reduction in demand is necessary. Consequently, one avoids sharp rises in unemployment, a swelling of the informal sector and large budget cuts. The greatest advantage of this policy is that it ensures a continuing flow of foreign capital before and during the adjustment period, instead of the complete cessation that occurs when adjustment is postponed until the crisis. This capital flow prevents a fall in private investment and public expenditure, which has socially unfavourable consequences.

How to Stabilize at Minimum Social Cost

In the light of all the simulations, it appears that devaluation is in general a more efficient and equitable instrument of stabilization than cutting public expenditure or the money supply. For a given reduction in the foreign deficit, a devaluation slows economic activity less and, as it is generally advantageous to the rural sector, leads to a better distribution of income and a decline in poverty.

Of course, public expenditure, fiscal policy and monetary policy can be altered to make the desired adjustment to an external shock, but the distributive effects of these changes are much less favourable. If stabilization measures are ranked by these effects, the two most costly would be increasing indirect taxation and laying off public employees, whereas a moderate cut in wages of public employees (if they are higher than other wages) would rank as the best. Our simulations, notably those for Indonesia and Morocco, also show that the definition of budgetary policies is very important. In the short and medium term, different results are obtained depending on which current expenditures and public investments are cut, especially if the social function of these expenditures is explicitly taken into account. For example, if investments are cut, those in rural areas, which will eventually increase peasant's incomes and reduce poverty, should be retained. If current expenditure is cut, this should not entail a cutback on medicines which would prevent the poor from obtaining hospital care.

It is clear that each government has a choice among many combinations of stabilization measures, as simulations show that various combinations of measures could lead to a given macroeconomic objective — for example, restoring the equilibrium of the balance of payments — while having different social costs and indirect effects. As each country has its specific characteristics, the government should draw up a socially optimal stabilization programme that takes these characteristics into account, instead of resorting to a standard programme.

It is also necessary, however, to take political constraints into account when formulating an adjustment policy, because the socially optimal programme could prove unfeasible for political reasons. In this respect, the Ecuadorian study and its use of a model are quite instructive. Some social objectives could be incompatible with constraints deriving from the politics of income distribution and redistribution. For example, the middle class or public employees could, as was seen in several countries, oppose measures exclusively targeted at the poor or the rural sector. In this case, the very notion of optimising should be discarded for a concept that is socially vaguer but politically more operational.

Advantages and Social Cost of Structural Adjustment

In principle, structural adjustment policies have so little effect on macroeconomic equilibria in the short term that it would be illusory to employ them for stabilization purposes. Some structural adjustment measures, however, have short term income-creating effects: price liberalisation in agriculture ordinarily benefits peasants, unless they have to buy agricultural products because of meagreness of their holdings. In this case, reconciling structural adjustment with equity requires rounding off this liberalisation by a change in the agrarian structure so that even small farms can have a surplus for the market.

The liberalisation of foreign trade, both imports and exports, has several effects on income creation. The abolition of quotas and reduction of customs tariffs hits owners of overprotected and inefficient businesses, as well as their workers, who have middle and high incomes. However, this policy lowers prices of manufactured goods relative to prices of agricultural products, which benefits peasants and decreases poverty when this predominates in rural areas. The balance sheet of liberalisation is thus rather favourable, as confirmed *a contrario* by a study on protectionism, which increases poverty and leads to a decline in average income of the poorest 60 per cent. In addition the growth of exports has favourable effects on the small and medium farmers if they are exporters, and in the non-agricultural sector it promotes expansion of labour-intensive industries, which reduces unemployment or underemployment in cities.

Structural adjustment has other favourable effects: certain measures result in a net social gain for some without losses for others. Furthermore, they increase the economy's flexibility. The costs of a stabilization programme turn out to be much lower when prices are flexible than when they are rigid. There is one structural adjustment measure, however, that has a large social cost: reorganising the public sector enterprises, whether this involves privatisations or internal reform. This measure leads to a great number of lay-offs, and when implemented during a stabilization programme, it could create explosive conditions in cities. Compensation programmes to aid the unemployed, as in Ghana, are therefore indispensable. In the immediate, it is necessary to ensure some sort of food safety net, then to reintegrate the unemployed in the economy, for example, by helping them become planters or artisans.

The Role of Donors

Donors have a determining role in reconciling adjustment and equity. First, they can persuade governments to act before a crisis occurs, for example, by proposing compensatory aid for certain groups, which could overcome the obstacles to an anticipated adjustment. If the crisis arrives, donors can reduce the social costs of stabilization in several ways. Their aid could perhaps be conditioned on the choice of an optimal programme, as determined by instruments such as the model described in this study. However, the most equitable programme is not always feasible politically. In this case, the donors' role is decisive, for when there is a budget deficit, they alone can finance transfers to the groups rejecting the programme and to the poor. In fact, even an equitable programme may increase poverty temporarily. If this social cost of adjustment is to be avoided, it is necessary to finance compensatory transfers equivalent to 1 to 4 per cent of GDP, which is not negligible, given the state of public finances.

Donors also have some responsibilities in case of structural adjustment: ensuring that liberalisation benefits small peasants, for example, and especially by participating in the financing of the safety net that is indispensable when state enterprises are reorganised. Of course, these steps could involve a large financial cost, but the donors can, by making it a condition of their loans, ensure that the adjustment policy is well conceived and efficiently implemented, so that these transfers rapidly (three or four years) cease to be necessary. These examples show that if donors really want to reduce the social costs of adjustment, they cannot simply express their good intentions and provide advice, but must become involved financially. However, the stakes — the political and social stability of many developing countries — justify this commitment by donors.

Chapter I

Disequilibria, Crisis and Adjustment

1. Disequilibria and Crisis

The developing countries on which the case studies focused had differing economic structures and performances before the arrival of the crisis which eventually resulted in an adjustment programme, and they also differed in the actual circumstances of the crisis. These differences are important since they could have caused the observed disparities in the macro- and microeconomic effects of (comparable) adjustment policies in the countries studied, disparities which of course will be at the heart of this work.

Certain general characteristics of these countries are given in Table I.1. By and large the figures refer to the early 1980s — there are three-year averages for 1979-81 or 1980-82 — or generally to the years preceding the implementation of adjustment policies. In some cases they may correspond to crisis situations, in fact justifying the adjustment policies adopted between 1981 and 1983, depending on the country.

The seven countries considered — three African, two Asian and two Latin American — represent a relatively wide range of levels of development. In the poorest, Ghana, the GDP per capita was $390; it was more than $1 650 in Malaysia and over $2 000 in Chile. It should be understood, however, that these figures are sometimes too large because some countries in the sample had currencies that were obviously overvalued. The GDP per capita ranking nonetheless represents structural differences usually associated with the development process: a definite predominance of the agricultural sector in the poorest countries and rapid growth of the manufacturing sector's share with gross output per capita. In this respect, the seven countries of the sample correspond to certain "types" commonly emphasized in development literature. Chile and Malaysia could be considered as semi-industrialised members of the middle-income countries. Ghana finds its place among the least favoured sub-Saharan economies, while Ecuador and Indonesia clearly represent the case of petroleum-exporting countries and, more generally, countries whose exports are highly dependent on a single product whose world market price is highly unstable.

The countries of the sample differed widely in their openness, as measured by the share of exports and/or imports in the GDP. Ghana is an exceptional case with a 7 per cent export ratio. To be sure, this figure may be largely underestimated, given the importance of contraband in this country, whose cocoa exports, the main component of foreign trade, are highly regulated. At the other extreme, foreign trade appears to dominate the Malaysian economy. Between these extremes, the degree of openness of the other five countries ranged from 22 to 38 per cent, figures typical of countries of modest size — although Indonesia is not in that category. Furthermore, it should be noted that by the beginning of the 1980s only Malaysia and Morocco had been able to export a significant volume of manufactured products. In the other countries, manufactures accounted for less than 10 per cent of total exports, during a period when raw material prices were already in decline and thus when that percentage should have been higher than the long term trend.

Given their strong correlation with the rates of growth by decade, the figures on public investment in Table I.1 are probably more representative of the 1970s than of the years just preceding the implementation of adjustment policies. From this point of view, the highest growth in the sample occurred in the petroleum-exporting countries (Ecuador, Indonesia and, to a lesser extent, Malaysia) and Côte d'Ivoire. The continuing economic decline of Ghana, which actually dates from the middle of the 1960s, is well known and is explained primarily by the gradual disappearance of incentives for the trading economy. Chile and Morocco are special cases, as the figures of Table I.1 hide great fluctuations. It is obvious that the decade of the 1970s is not representative of Chile's actual potential for growth. The 1973 coup d'état followed an unusual economic situation; just as exceptional were the successive, highly important liberal reforms of 1974-76, while the economic boom was, to a large extent, simply a recovery from the preceding period. The 4.2 per cent annual rate of growth shown in the table represents an average between two disparate periods. Likewise, it should be noted that the Moroccan economic crisis and adjustment policies date back to 1978, shortly after the collapse of the price of phosphates, which had tripled in 1973-74. For various reasons, especially social, these adjustment programmes could not be implemented without interruption until 1983. It follows that Morocco's average annual rate of growth in the 1970s greatly underestimates the economy's potential for growth and appears inconsistent with the extremely large share of investment in the GDP.

The causes of the crisis that necessitates adjustment, if not the crisis itself, can already be seen in some countries' budget deficits and current account deficits at the beginning of the 1980s. The majority of the sample — the exceptions are the two Asian economies — had large deficits in the balance of trade, though this concept is almost without meaning for Ghana, given its closed economy. Again except for the two Asian countries and Ghana, the current account deficit, or equivalently the shortfall of domestic savings for investment, ranged between one-third and three-fourths of export receipts, or between 8 and 15 per cent of GDP. Furthermore, the budget deficit represents a sizeable share of GDP in several countries: 6 per cent in Ghana, 8 per cent in Malaysia, 10 per cent in Côte d'Ivoire and 12 per cent in Morocco; the last figure indicates that Morocco was already deep in crisis at the beginning of the 1980s. It is nevertheless true that Chile registered a budget surplus, while Ecuador and Indonesia had only a small deficit.

In most of the countries which had large budget and current account deficits, a major cause was the interest payments on the foreign debt accumulated in the 1970s, which had financed a part of the public investments in that period. This debt was very large even in countries like Ghana and Indonesia, which did not have current account difficulties at the beginning of the 1980s. Indonesia's substantial balance-of-payments surplus enabled it to make debt service payments without becoming more indebted, while in Ghana the interest on the debt was very low. In fact, among the countries of the sample only Malaysia had been able to avoid the mounting indebtedness of the 1970s. Such a build-up did occur but it was confined to the domestic market. Apart from Malaysia, Table I.1 shows that the total (private and public) foreign debt of the countries of the sample is equivalent to export receipts of a year or more. The corresponding interest payments range from 6 to 18 per cent of export receipts (excluding Ghana and Malaysia), or from 1.8 to 3.6 per cent of GDP.

Inflation will be our last indicator of the health of these economies before the turbulent developments of the 1980s. Four countries experienced high rates of inflation which in one way or another resulted in tension over the division of the national product among the factors of production or between the public and private sectors. This occurred in the two Latin American countries (Chile and Ecuador), Ghana and Indonesia.

Given the conditions just described, how were these economies affected by the main economic events occurring around 1980? In the first place, there was a deterioration of the terms of trade. As shown in Table I.1, the fall in prices of copper in Chile, of coffee and cocoa in Côte d'Ivoire and Ghana, of rubber and other products in Malaysia resulted in a 14 to 25 per cent decline in the terms of trade, depending on the country, in the first two years of the crisis. The impact of this fall obviously depends on the extent of the economy's openness. In Malaysia, where exports accounted for more than 50 per cent of GDP, a 14 per cent fall in the terms of trade caused a decrease in external purchasing power of more than 7 per cent of GDP, and thus of the real domestic income of the economy. The shock was of a similar order of magnitude in Côte d'Ivoire and about 3 per cent of GDP in Chile. The deterioration of the terms of trade did not necessarily coincide with the crisis which would trigger the adjustment programme. Morocco's phosphate prices had already begun to fall in 1978. The large fall in Ecuador's petroleum prices began in 1983, when an adjustment policy had already been launched. Finally, when Côte d'Ivoire and Ghana experienced a deterioration of the terms of trade in 1982, they had already suffered a similar decline in 1980, the first drop in coffee and cocoa prices after the boom of 1976.

A second external factor explaining the major economic crisis around 1982-83 in the countries of the sample was the evolution of the international capital market. Two related phenomena in this domain had a great impact in the second half of 1982: the increase in interest rates and a scarcity of international credit. For the sample countries that had large foreign debts and for those experiencing balance-of-trade difficulties — because of the drop in the terms of trade, for example — the consequences were catastrophic: a considerable increase in the weight of interest payments in the current account and, in some cases, a contraction of economic activity resulting from inability to borrow abroad. Table I.1 shows that interest charges almost doubled in the space of two years for Chile, Côte d'Ivoire, Ghana and Malaysia. Furthermore, all the countries did not necessarily acquit the totality of their debt service in those years, thereby justifying the intervention of the IMF and the implementation of an adjustment programme.

Sudden changes in the terms of trade and conditions for borrowing abroad would not necessarily have provoked a major crisis in most of the sample countries, if they had not occurred in a situation that was already unstable. From this point of view, it is evident that the large foreign indebtedness incurred by almost all of these countries in the 1970s has been fraught with consequences. The domestic political factors or errors responsible for this indebtedness must therefore be considered among the causes of the crisis which led to a more or less drastic readjustment of the economies of these countries.

In the first place, one should probably mention the expectations — incorrect *a posteriori* — based on the boom in raw material prices in the mid-1970s. In the countries of the sample, the boom affected petroleum (Ecuador, Indonesia and Malaysia), copper (Chile), coffee and cocoa (Côte d'Ivoire and Ghana), rubber (Malaysia) and phosphates (Morocco). The boom was ordinarily interpreted as a permanent improvement in the terms of trade; it was thus natural that governments borrowed abroad in order to augment capital outlays (thereby accelerating exploitation of the boom) and to distribute part of the gains of future growth, especially since conditions on the international credit market were quite favourable at that epoch. Policies of this sort were adopted, in differing degrees, by Côte d'Ivoire, Ecuador, Indonesia, Malaysia and Morocco. Since these expectations were incorrect — we will not discuss in detail how they arose or the corresponding spending policies — they must be considered as errors of economic policy whose consequences were exceedingly grave in some cases.

In several countries these variations of foreign prices were accompanied by other distortions. In particular, economic policy makers had been slow to react to symptoms of the "Dutch disease", which was caused by a relative increase in prices of non-tradable goods and of the real exchange rate. This resulted in an allocation of productive resources which was revealed inadequate when the terms of trade fell. This phenomenon has been particularly marked in Ecuador, Côte d'Ivoire and Morocco. In several countries, moreover, projects involving large public investment undertaken in the euphoria of the 1970s have proved inefficient or low in productivity. The two Asian countries of the sample appear to have been less affected by such difficulties than the others.

The preceding explanation of the crisis and adjustment in the sample countries is particularly linked to external factors which gave rise to false expectations (or hopes): favourable terms of trade and conditions for international credit in the 1970s, a sudden reversal of these trends and an international liquidity crisis at the beginning of the 1980s. The economic policy errors relating to exchange management and the allocation and productivity of public investment are in some degree also related to these external factors. In the sample, Indonesia and Malaysia illustrate the first factors, while Côte d'Ivoire, Ecuador and Morocco illustrate the whole set of external factors.

In Morocco, however, additional internal weaknesses were also responsible for the situation at the beginning of the 1980s, before an adjustment programme was initiated. The same is true for Chile and Ghana although their weaknesses fell into completely different domains. Thus the crisis was as much internal as external in these three countries.

Morocco's terms of trade fell in 1978. An adjustment quickly appeared unavoidable, and on two occasions, in 1978 and 1981, a plan was formulated. In each case, the government's policy (elimination of price subsidies for food products and a pay freeze) came up against the interests of the middle and working classes in such a way that the adjustment had to be suspended. A drought occurring in 1981 also was in large measure responsible for the check of the second plan.

The external factors that led to Chile's 1982-83 crisis seem to have been intensified by two internal factors. On the one hand, the policy of pre-announced nominal devaluation rates put into effect as from 1979 to quash inflationary expectations and reduce inflation (*tablita*), achieved its aim, but it was accompanied by a significant overvaluation of the currency and a deterioration of the current account. On the other hand, the liberalisation of international capital movements led to a large increase in private indebtedness. This improvement in the capital account concealed difficulties of the current account. This raises the question of whether the sudden opening of the capital market, which modified the macroeconomic "closure" of the economy, was not the major factor in the economy's weakness at the time of the external shock of 1982.

Lastly, the case of Ghana is radically different from the others, although it too was greatly affected by the external shock of the 1980s, like all the countries of the sample. The difference resides in the almost continuous economic decline, whose main cause was purely internal, experienced by Ghana since the mid-1960s. Primarily for political reasons, an authoritarian government instituted a price system which, in the course of time, led prices increasingly far from their market levels. The result was a gradual disappearance of incentives for all actors involved in commerce: decline in cocoa production and in the share marketed by the state export organisation, fall of GDP, etc. A desire for reform and a return to a market economy appeared at the beginning of the 1980s, but this could not be achieved without substantial foreign aid because of the external shocks appearing at the same time.

This analysis of the crisis shows that the meaning of "crisis" depends on the country. Ecuador and Morocco are "classic" examples of crisis: the current account deficit increases for the reasons mentioned and the countries can no longer borrow. In this frozen situation at the end of 1983, both countries obtained loans from the IMF and introduced stabilization programmes. The only alternative would have been a drastic reduction of imports by the use of quotas, which the two countries had to do at the beginning of 1983. However, that measure has worse effects on economic activity and incomes, including those of the poor, than does a stabilization programme, as shown by a simulation with the macro-micro model applied to Morocco (see Chapter IV).

In other countries, however, the situation could be quite different from the classic case. In a sense, Ghana was no more in crisis in 1983 than five years earlier; more precisely, the economy had been ruined since the beginning of the 1970s, imports being very low because of the level of exports and the many years without loans. Having rejected adjustment, Ghana illustrates fairly well the consequences of the other alternative: increasingly strict rationing of imports within the framework of a self-centred "development" policy. Ghanaian officials decided to change the policy in 1983, but they should have made this decision earlier — or later. Indonesia is also a special case, but in a totally different context. The deterioration of the terms of trade in 1983 led of course to a fall in receipts and an increase in the external deficit. At that date, the situation was not catastrophic and the country could, by borrowing, have deferred adjustment for a year or more. Actually the fall in the price of petroleum to $12 the barrel occurred only in 1986. At that time, if there had not been an earlier adjustment, Indonesia would have been confronted with the same impasse as Morocco in 1983. By reacting very rapidly, the government forestalled this classic crisis. To some extent the case of Malaysia could be likened to that of Indonesia. Admittedly, the disequilibria there in 1984 were greater than those in Indonesia in 1983, but since this country was not heavily indebted, it probably could have borrowed and thus deferred the stabilization programme for one or two years.

This comparison shows that adjustment can be undertaken outside the classic case of crisis, either **before** or **after** this critical moment. Beforehand, it is a question of a difficult situation rather than a crisis, properly speaking, and governments have a margin of manoeuvre that they will not have afterwards. In the two examples cited, it is significant that the adjustment was carried out without the participation of the IMF. In adjusting before a crisis, a country has a freer choice of the programme's components and schedule; it works in an atmosphere of calm rather than an emergency. By contrast, when adjustment comes after the crisis recourse to the IMF becomes inevitable, for the country's financial situation is so bad that it cannot borrow from any commercial bank. When it goes to the IMF, the country renounces the self-centred development strategy adopted at the onset of the crisis of cutting imports to eliminate a deficit it can no longer finance.

These comments show the importance of the date of adjustment. At different times the possible choices are not the same. Furthermore, the longer a country waits, the more the disequilibria increase and the longer, more costly will be the stabilization process.

2. Stabilization and Structural Adjustment

The word **stabilization** evokes a simple image in the media: that of a country in financial crisis, which has to accept the IMF's conditions to reduce its external deficit and obtain more loans.

This picture conceals a reality that is more complex. First, the term **adjustment** corresponds to two different categories of measures, one to lessen total demand, the other to stimulate supply. Second, some developing countries, like Indonesia and Malaysia in the sample studied here, have embarked on an adjustment programme without an accord with the IMF.

To prevent any confusion, the term **stabilization** will be reserved for measures concerning demand and **structural adjustment** for supply policies. Stabilization programmes respond to a financial crisis: demand is decreased to reduce or even eliminate the external current account deficit. They involve measures for an urgent situation which should have effects in the short term (6 to 18 months). By contrast, a structural adjustment programme is for the medium to long term and is composed of a set of measures capable of increasing supply. When these measures have a financial cost — for example, when customs duties are reduced or there is investment in agriculture — sometimes the World Bank accords loans to finance them. Some measures, however, have both stabilizing and structural effects. For example, a devaluation reduces total demand and restructures productive sectors.

Although stabilization and structural adjustment should be distinguished, they are nonetheless based on a common logic. Both treat the same illness, one by curative action, the other by preventive action. In fact, the disequilibria which led to a financial crisis stem in part from insufficient domestic supply with respect to demand. Once equilibrium has been re-established by the stabilization programme, the best means of avoiding new imbalances is to increase productive capacity. In addition, the insufficient domestic supply is in part attributable to unsuitable economic structures: for example, an inefficient public sector in deficit, overprotected industries oriented towards the domestic market, or agricultural prices which discourage production. Therefore, the structural adjustment consists of a reform in depth of the economy to change the framework in which enterprises function. Such a reform has favourable consequences for some interest groups and unfavourable ones for others. It thus corresponds to a change in a country's socio-political equilibrium, which is easier to make acceptable in a crisis situation and with a stabilization programme. This has been verified for both developing and industrialised countries, as shown by the stabilization programme and structural adjustment carried out in France in 1958. In this sense, stabilization and structural adjustment are linked for both economic and political reasons. This linkage is evident when the IMF and World Bank work together to persuade governments that stabilization measures should be accompanied by structural reforms. Obviously, the reforms do not have the same urgency as stabilization and it takes time to formulate them. That explains the interval between implementing a stabilization programme and obtaining loans for structural adjustment. For example, the World Bank granted such loans to Morocco in March 1984 and July 1985, although the accord with the IMF had been made in September 1983. The Ivoirien stabilization programme of January 1981 was followed by a structural adjustment loan in December 1981.

Stabilization programmes

The shock treatment represented by all stabilization programmes consists of the same measures in most cases: total demand is reduced by cuts in public expenditure and also by a devaluation and a reduction of the money supply. If it is not possible to devalue, export subsidies and an increase in import duties have, in principle, the same effect as a devaluation. In reality, this alternative policy may fail, as was seen in Côte d'Ivoire in 1987, when it resulted in a rapid development of smuggling.

Budget cuts under a stabilization programme always have a greater effect on public investment than on current expenditure. There are several reasons for this. First, in the period of expansion preceding the crisis, public investment had increased the most rapidly. It thus appears that capital outlays are being sacrificed because a comparison is made with the previous year rather than with five or ten years earlier. Second, the exterior deficit is the determining constraint; cutting public investment is thus preferable to cutting current expenditure because it procures a greater reduction of imports. Finally, public opinion is less sensitive to cuts in capital outlays than of current expenditure. Public investment consists primarily of public works. Reductions in this domain affect a disparate population of small entrepreneurs and workers with minimal skills, while a reduction of current expenditure would affect groups most likely to react, such as public employees who are laid off or students whose grants are cut. Of course, the fall in public investment will have negative effects (deterioration of infrastructure and lowering of productivity of private investment), but these developments become evident only after a more or less long time; straightaway they entail neither dangerous anti-governmental political reactions nor economic effects that are too visible.

Cuts in public investment caused by a stabilization programme were striking in countries like Côte d'Ivoire and Morocco, which had the most ambitious policies in the preceding years. Public investment had tripled in Morocco between 1965-67 and 1978-80. It declined 38 per cent between 1983 and 1986. In Côte d'Ivoire, capital outlays by the state and public enterprises increased from 15 to 21 per cent of GDP between 1975 and 1978. The first stabilization programme in 1981 cut this percentage in half; after an increase in 1982-83, a second programme limited it to 7.5 per cent. Similar developments can be seen in Ecuador: a sharp increase from 1979 to 1981 from 5.3 to 7.3 per cent of GDP after the second petroleum shock, followed by as steep a cut, to 4.4 per cent in 1984. In Indonesia and Malaysia, the cuts were more moderate, amounting to 11 percent (in volume) between 1983 and 1984 for Indonesia and from 1983 to 1986 for Malaysia. Given the sizeable increases before these stabilization measures, the level of public investment still remained much higher than several years earlier; by comparison with 1980, it was 16 per cent higher in Indonesia in 1984 and 67 per cent higher in Malaysia in 1986. Thus in the medium term of four to five years, there had been no cut in these two countries.

Change in the opposite direction is also possible, as in Ghana. In this country, gradually ruined by disastrous economic policies, public investment had collapsed before the 1983 stabilization programme began, falling from 7 per cent of GDP in 1975 to less than 1 per cent in 1982, before rising to 2 per cent in 1985, owing to this programme. In the event, the context is completely different since Ghana, unlike the other countries, suffered a drop in its foreign currency receipts prior to 1983. The return to imports and later to public investment was only made possible through loans linked to the stabilisation programme.

While one of the customary components of a stabilization programme is a reduction of public investment, there exist exceptions and in the medium term investment can continue to increase, as in Indonesia and Malaysia.

By contrast, government current expenditure proves to be rather rigid. Of course, stabilization programmes can reduce them, but not by much. In Indonesia they dropped by 1.7 per cent between 1983 and 1984, and in Malaysia by 4.6 per cent between 1983 and 1986. In Ecuador there was also a small drop in absolute terms and as a percentage of a stagnant GDP, from 24 per cent in 1980-82 to 21 per cent in 1984. In Chile, however, the first stabilization programme (1983-84) did not entail any cut in current expenditure; this occurred only in 1986-87 (-2 per cent each year) during the second programme. Lastly, in Côte d'Ivoire current expenditure rose both as a percentage of GDP and, to a lesser extent, in absolute terms. Similarly, in Morocco it increased slightly as a percentage of GDP from 1982 to 1985 and returned to its initial level in 1986.

Current expenditures as a whole thus appear rather stable: stabilization programmes stop their growth, but never make drastic cuts. Nevertheless, measures to stabilize or reduce current expenditure are delicate because of their political implications. In fact, wages are the main expenditure, and subsidies often account for a large share of the other expenditures; governments that stabilize current expenditure must therefore cut the real pay of state employees and/or subsidies.

In Côte d'Ivoire, nominal wages were frozen in 1981 and the freeze was maintained in 1983 and 1984. In Côte d'Ivoire and Morocco the pay freeze resulted in a fall of real wages. Likewise, the Indonesian government froze nominal wages in 1986. In Chile, real wages were reduced between 1983 and 1986 by 13 to 17 per cent with respect to their 1980-81 level.

The other measure that stabilizes or reduces the payroll is to slow recruitment, even to lay off. In 1984, the Ivoirien government reduced new enrolment by 25 per cent in schools which trained students for public employment. In Morocco recruiting was reduced from 40 000 to 25 000 per year. Nonetheless, public employment continued to increase during the stabilization period (by 50 000 from 1982 to 1986). By contrast, in Chile the number of public employees did not change from 1982 to 1985. Ghana took the most far-reaching measures: the stabilization programme provided for reducing personnel 5 per cent a year by lay-offs. This objective was not attained, but by 1988, 12 000 public employees had been dismissed, with an equal number of lay-offs in the Cocoa Marketing Board, the main public enterprise.

Except in Ghana governments tried to stabilize the public payroll — which increases automatically, because of promotions and seniority, even when the number of employees is constant — without resorting to harsh measures like lay-offs and reducing nominal wages, because of the political importance of public employees. That explains the preference for "mild" measures: freezing of nominal wages or reducing recruitment.

Measures were also taken to reduce subsidies, despite the considerable political risk. This entailed reducing direct consumer subsidies or raising the prices charged by public utilities (energy, transport, etc.) to eliminate state subsidies. Thus in Morocco subsidies were eliminated on certain foodstuffs (on butter and milk in 1983, on high-quality wheat in 1985), while not changing those on basic foodstuffs (oil, sugar and medium-quality wheat). In addition, there were increases in the prices of electricity, water and transport. In Côte d'Ivoire the rates for these public utilities were increased and the subsidy on rice was reduced in 1981. There were further rate increases for the utilities and a reduction of the housing subsidy for public employees in 1984. The Indonesian government cut the subsidy on fertilizer in half from 1982 to 1985. Likewise, Ghana reduced the subsidies on fertilizers and insecticides, with the aim of eliminating them by 1990. In Chile, the stabilization programme included price increases on services.

These measures were similar to reductions in public expenditure for education and health. Thus in Ghana costs of medical consultations and the daily charge for hospitalisation were raised, purchase of school textbooks was instituted and subsidies for student meals and lodging were reduced. In Côte d'Ivoire, the second stabilization programme in 1984 entailed reducing the number of grants by one-half for higher education and by one-third for secondary education. Similarly, Morocco made the criteria for student grants more selective.

23

Like cuts in public expenditure, monetary policy is an essential part of all stabilization programmes. That is obvious in countries with perennial inflation, as in Latin America. Thus in Ecuador a ceiling was imposed on credits for the public sector. The 1983 stabilization programme also provided for tightening private sector credit, which fell steadily from 30.6 per cent of GDP in 1983 to 23.4 per cent in 1987. Furthermore, the growth of the money supply (M1) was limited, the M1/GDP ratio falling from 0.14 in 1983 to 0.12 in 1987. In Chile, liquidity of the economy was reduced beginning in 1982, before the stabilization programme, because it had been decided to make the money supply vary with the reserves of foreign exchange, which fell rapidly in 1982 as a result of capital flight.

The other countries also made use of monetary policy. Côte d'Ivoire's 1981 stabilization programme provided for slowing the growth of domestic credit, as did Morocco's in 1983. In Ghana, which had experienced hyper-inflation, growth of the money supply fell from 49 per cent in 1983 to 18 per cent in 1984. Indonesia's monetary officials slowed the growth of the money supply, while freeing interest rates so that households would increase their term deposits. Finally, in Malaysia the size of the money supply remained stable in 1984 and 1985 after growing more than 10 per cent annually in preceding years. Thus it is clear that all stabilization implies a tight money policy which varies only in form, depending upon the institutional context.

The same holds for foreign exchange policy: each programme provides for a devaluation to slow domestic consumption (provided that money policy is restrictive), encourage exports and restructure demand to the benefit of domestic goods. This option is not possible, however, for countries that belong to a monetary zone; in our sample, Côte d'Ivoire could not devalue because it belongs to the franc zone. This drawback was fortunately offset by the devaluation of the French franc three times from 1981 to 1983, yet this advantage in turn was limited by the fact that a large share of Ivoirien exports go to France.

Indonesia devalued the rupiah by 28 per cent in 1983 and adopted a floating rate of exchange roughly linked to the dollar. When the petroleum price fell again, the government carried out another devaluation of 31 per cent in 1986. After appreciation of its currency until 1984, Malaysia let the ringgit depreciate beginning in 1985, so that the effective real rate of exchange fell by 30 per cent in two years. After having already devalued its currency 23 per cent, in March 1983 Ecuador announced a series of mini-devaluations of 3 per cent a month. In 1985, most foreign transactions made at the official rate were transferred to the free market, with the result that the sucre went from 66.5 to 95 to the dollar. Finally, there was another devaluation in February 1986. Chile, after an appreciation of its currency in 1981, carried out a series of devaluations beginning in 1982, which lowered the real rate of exchange 10 to 20 per cent a year until 1985.

Among the sample countries it was in Ghana that the greatest overvaluation occurred, with two consequences: rationing of imports and a very active parallel market for foreign currency. The stabilization programme therefore involved a major devaluation in which the dollar rose from 2.75 cedis at the beginning of 1983 to 90 cedis in 1986. After that depreciation failed to re-establish equilibrium on the foreign exchange market, in September 1986, at the time of the third IMF loan, an auction system was introduced for most foreign transactions, except for cocoa sales and purchases of petroleum and medicines. On this market, the dollar attained 154 cedis at the end of 1986, and the discrepancy with the parallel market, which exceeded 10 to 1 before the adjustment, fell to 20 per cent.

Structural adjustment programmes

While stabilization programmes pursue a single objective by a single set of measures, structural adjustment involves greater variety. Its aim of increasing economic efficiency means something different for each country. In-depth reform and privatisation of a part of the public sector are indispensable when this is large and inefficient, but they are not necessary when this sector is small and/or well-managed. It may be desirable to reform agricultural prices if they are fixed by the state at a low level which discourages the producers, but not if the state limits its intervention to judicious operations to stabilize prices. Thus the structural reforms necessary for overcoming dysfunctional situations and inappropriate regulations vary greatly from country to country. Each structural adjustment programme should respond to a specific problem of the country concerned. Nevertheless, as all the experience cited shows, these programmes are imbued with a common philosophy when they are drawn up with the World Bank: the advantage of liberalisation of all trade, both domestic and foreign, and possibly the advantage of privatising part of the public sector, to make the economy more efficient. This was also the philosophy of countries like Indonesia, acting independently of the World Bank (which does not exclude informal consultation).

In countries like Indonesia, Malaysia and Chile, where the agricultural sector was regulated by the market, liberalisation was unnecessary. By contrast, liberalisation measures have been carried out in Morocco, Côte d'Ivoire and especially Ghana, where prices were highly distorted. In Morocco, the government increased the producer prices of regulated products and the fees for water, while reducing subsidies on fertilizers. In addition, the state has allowed private enterprises to sell fertilizer and to produce and sell seeds, and it has ended the public monopoly for agricultural exports. Côte d'Ivoire has taken comparable steps: raised the producer price of rice and cotton, aligned the price of rubber with the world market price, abolished subsidies on fertilizer for cotton and privatised state enterprises which process and market rice. These measures were supported by the World Bank, which accorded a structural adjustment loan to Côte d'Ivoire and a loan to Morocco specifically for financing agricultural investments.

Liberalisation has brought the most changes to Ghana. Between 1983 and 1987 there was a seven-fold increase in the producer price of cocoa to bring it in line with the world market price. The Cocoa Marketing Board (or Cocobod) has been reorganised to decrease its margin, and part of its activities have been privatised (plantations and means of transport). The personnel have been reduced by 40 per cent because of evident overstaffing (102 000 as compared with several thousand in 1960 when production was much higher). The World Bank wanted further privatisation and greater reduction of personnel, but the government moderated this project because of employee resistance and the private sector's limited capacity. Prices of other agricultural products have also been raised, while subsidies were lowered on fertilizers, insecticides and pesticides.

All these measures in these three countries had the same objective: re-establishing true prices in agriculture and abolishing state monopolies on the provision of inputs and marketing, using privatisation policies as the means of liberalising prices.

The same policy of getting the prices right is also applied in the non-agricultural sector. In Ghana state control of prices had been the most far-reaching. The Prices and Incomes Board, established in 1972, fixed the prices of most goods and gave its accord for all pay increases. Prices were liberalised beginning in 1984, and from 1985 on the state limited its control of prices to eight goods. This reform entailed the ending of subsidies on some goods. In contrast, Morocco conserved a market economy but the state nonetheless controlled the prices of many goods and services. Under the structural reform programme all controls were abolished for 60 categories of goods. In addition, authorisation of accelerated amortizing was ended, thus raising the cost of capital significantly in relation to labour, after the sharp fall in the 1970s had encouraged enterprises to use more capital-intensive techniques. Morocco also instituted financial liberalisation: nominal interest rates were raised so that real rates would become positive, and various steps were taken to encourage savings.

This financial liberalisation was also chosen by Indonesia. Before 1983, the government fixed interest rates and decided on the allocation of credit. A major reform of the banking system in 1983 abolished ceilings on interest rates for borrowing and lending, as well as measures for rationing credit. Loans at subsidised interest rates were ended and a capital market was established. These measures are based on the same logic as liberalisation of industrial prices since they bring interest rates closer to their equilibrium value.

Liberalisation of foreign trade, the second facet of adjustment programmes, has perhaps the greatest structural effects. It significantly reduces the protection given to import-substitution industries and encourages industries to turn more towards the exterior in accordance with their comparative advantage.

Morocco provides the best example since it received the first structural adjustment loan for financing this new policy. All export duties and exporting licenses were abolished in 1984. The import quotas imposed during the financial crisis at the beginning of 1983 were dismantled. In addition, import duties, which went as high as 400 per cent, were reduced to a maximum of 45 per cent. As a result the average rate of imposition (all duties included) dropped by one-half between 1983 and 1986. Côte d'Ivoire undertook similar actions in the framework of structural adjustment: abolishing import quotas, unifying and lowering import duties to leave an effective average rate of protection of 40 per cent on domestic manufactured products. The reform of external trade had major significance for Ghana since all imports had been rationed. At the beginning, quotas were maintained but importers could freely import goods for which they had the foreign currency. In 1986 quotas on raw materials, spare parts and capital goods were abolished. This measure was later extended to most other goods and import duties were reduced to a moderate level.

Changes in other countries were much less spectacular since their economies had not been cut off from the exterior like Ghana's, yet these countries implemented the same policy. In 1985, Indonesia reduced the number and level of tariffs, the highest being cut from 225 to 60 per cent. In 1986, enterprises which exported their products were authorised to import intermediate goods without limit or duty. Then in 1986-87, import licenses were abolished for many goods, with the result that the share of imports subject to licensing declined from 43 per cent in 1986 to 21 per cent in 1988. In addition, all export licenses were abolished. In Chile, where imports had already been liberalised, the structural adjustment loan accorded by the World Bank helped to finance the promotion of exports: development of a forestry programme and aid for non-mining exports (moreover, the exchange rate was maintained at a level favourable to these exporters). Likewise Ecuador liberalised exports by abolishing taxes and licenses, but it increased protective duties on imports — an exception in this listing of trade liberalisation.

All the cited countries put into effect measures to promote exports. If we bear in mind that each structural adjustment programme involves one or more devaluations, it is clear that the main objective of adjustment in the medium to long term is reorienting and restructuring economies towards the exterior markets that should promote growth, the antithesis of the self-centred development model illustrated by Ghana, which had the disastrous consequences that have been described.

In the Asian and Latin American countries studied the size of state enterprises was modest; thus their management did not involve macroeconomic problems as in Morocco, Côte d'Ivoire and especially Ghana. For the latter group, reforming the public sector was a precondition of re-establishing budget equilibrium because of the major role of these enterprises in the modern sector and problems of their management, which entailed large state-financed deficits. For example, in Ghana these deficits amounted to 16 per cent of government spending in 1983. Thus structural adjustment plans for each country provided for reforming these enterprises. In Morocco, the government prepared some privatisations and drew up a programme with the World Bank to improve the performance of these enterprises and clarify their relations with the state. In Côte d'Ivoire, a more ambitious programme was undertaken: closing or privatising enterprises, control of borrowing, audits of management, reorganisation and financial reform. In Ghana, where the state enterprises controlled the majority of the modern sector, a preparatory study for structural reform recommended closing or privatising 80 out of 230 enterprises. Beginning in 1987, these recommendations were put into effect, slowly to be sure, given the difficulty of finding buyers and some opposition within the government. In other respects, the public sector was reformed in depth: gradual ending of subsidies, personnel reductions, equality of competition with private enterprise and limits on access to bank credits. A listing of these measures reveals that the main issue is not privatisation, but a management conforming to the rules of a market economy, whether that management results from internal reforms or privatisation.

This observation underscores the common objective of all these structural adjustment measures to restore or establish a market economy, considered essential to improve efficiency and, consequently, output in the medium term. Furthermore, a decision to stabilize, like devaluation, is based on the same logic. Usually a crisis is accompanied by an inflation due the financing of the budget deficit by creation of money. As a result of this inflation and in the absence of automatic correction of the rate of exchange, the currency is overvalued and thus a devaluation can be interpreted as an operation of getting the prices right: the exchange rate is brought down to its market equilibrium value. This reasoning could be extended to certain budgetary and monetary stabilization measures, for strict monetary and budgetary policy is based on the same philosophy.

This re-establishment or strengthening of the market mechanism obviously requires a more or less long period. In the short term, the only observable effects of adjustment are those of the stabilization measures. Interpreting the macroeconomic data is nevertheless delicate because the latter reflect both the stabilization policy and the financial crisis which preceded it.

3. The Economic Consequences of Stabilization Measures

The first criterion of success of these measures is a reduction of the current account deficit. A comparison of the deficits in the two years before and the two following a stabilization programme indicates success in most countries. Sometimes success is striking as in Ecuador and Malaysia, where the deficit passed from 10 per cent of GDP to equilibrium. The improvement for the other countries was quite significant, with the exception of Côte d'Ivoire, where the deficit did not diminish. This failure is explained by the drought of 1983, which affected exports and compelled the country to reschedule its debt and undertake a new stabilization programme. It may also be noted that the performance of the two countries that adjusted on their own, Indonesia and Malaysia, was on average as good as that of the other countries.

The first question raised by these performances is what they cost in terms of growth. In fact, stabilization programmes are generally associated with the negative image of recessions. Contrary to this view, in four out of the seven countries the rate of GDP growth was **higher** in the two years following stabilization than in the two years preceding. Furthermore, among the three countries in which growth decreased there was only one case of recession, that of Côte d'Ivoire (with a rate of -4.1 per cent), while in Indonesia the slowing of growth was small. An observation of even greater significance is that the rate of GDP growth was equal to or greater than 3 per cent in all the countries except Malaysia and Côte d'Ivoire. Taking demographic increase into account, that means that per capita GDP declined in only two of the seven countries. This result is very important because changes in poverty are highly dependent on changes in the GDP per capita. This comparison between the two years before and the two following an adjustment is nonetheless biased because the macroeconomic disequilibria slowed growth in the first period. It would thus be preferable to use a longer reference period, which we have done by considering the seven years before the adjustment. However, this does not substantially change the results: growth still remains higher in three of the four countries of the first comparison, although the differences between the rates before and after adjustment clearly decrease. Of the four countries, only in Morocco was the rate of growth in the seven-year period before the adjustment higher than in the two subsequent years, but the difference was very small (0.3 per cent).

We must qualify this appraisal, however, by recalling the unusual circumstances of some countries before the year of stabilization. In 1982, Chile went through its gravest crisis with a fall in GDP of 15 per cent, a crisis due to the combination of economic policy errors with unfavourable exogenous shocks (increase in the international lending rate and fall in the terms of trade). When Ghana embarked on a stabilization programme, it was immersed in a grave long-term crisis since the GDP per capita had fallen 30 per cent between 1971-74 and 1982, the crisis being characterised by insufficient supply and not, as is usually the case, by excess demand. If we compare the stabilization programmes of Morocco and Côte d'Ivoire, it is certain that the results would have been completely different if the climatic conditions of the two countries during the stabilization period had been reversed.

This qualified record indicates that reality is more complex than a simple overheating of the economy (with excess demand and increasing external deficit), which precedes and explains the adjustment and the fall in activity. In some countries, like Ghana and Chile, adjustment follows a grave crisis; in other cases

27

the results of an adjustment are greatly influenced by weather conditions, which can be expected in a country where agriculture accounts for a large share of employment and exports.

Since the aim of stabilization programmes is re-establishing basic equilibria, two other criteria of success are reducing the budget deficit and the rate of inflation, but they are secondary criteria because reduction of this deficit is a means of reducing the external deficit and not an end in itself.

All the countries had a serious external deficit before the adjustment. The effect of the stabilization programmes depended on the country. The deficit fell in most of the countries, to the point where there was a surplus in Ecuador and, in 1986, Ghana. It increased in Chile, however, and remained nearly constant in Côte d'Ivoire, owing to the fall in exports and receipts from them. If those random fluctuations are excluded, it can be concluded that the stabilization programmes succeeded in partly or completely eliminating the external deficit since it really was not a problem in Chile.

By contrast, not all the countries had a budget deficit. In some cases it was negligible as a percentage of GDP, for example, -0.6 per cent in Chile and -2 per cent in Indonesia. When there was a large budget deficit, the stabilization programme did reduce it, but this success is less evident than for the external deficit, and in some countries like Morocco a significant budget deficit remained.

All the countries studied experienced inflationary tensions before the stabilization programmes, with rates exceeding 10 per cent, except in Malaysia. As a consequence of these programmes the rates of inflation fell, except those of Chile and Ecuador, which increased sharply because the growth of the money supply had not been controlled. In Ecuador, the rate of inflation rose from 16 per cent in 1982-83 to 42 per cent in 1984. It should also be recalled that from 1982-83 a deflationary trend in industrialised countries encouraged the fall of inflation in most of the countries undergoing adjustment.

In all the countries there was a large increase in foreign debt. The ratio of the debt to GDP doubling on average in less than five years, owing to the increase in interest rates and to the new loans that all adjustment programmes authorise after a financial crisis. The new policies in Malaysia and Indonesia enabled their governments to obtain new loans easily even without an accord with the IMF. The debt service/exports and debt/GDP ratios of these two countries moved in parallel. In the other countries, however, the first ratio increased much less than the second, or even decreased, as a result of the stabilization programme because the accords with the IMF rescheduled the debt.

It is therefore possible to define the constant effects of these programmes: they all led in the short term to a sharp reduction of the external deficit and, with the exceptions noted, of the budget deficit and rate of inflation, at the price of growth in debt but not in debt service (if there is an accord with the IMF). Moreover, there was relatively little effect on economic activity during this period, although growth slowed in two cases and GDP decreased in one. As the level of economic activity depends on other factors besides the stabilization measures, however, this slowing is not the consequence and cost of adjustment alone. This cost, other things being equal, can be evaluated only by models, as will be seen in Chapter IV. At the end of that chapter, some simulations based on other stabilization programmes, or on policies of "non-adjustment" with import rationing, show how different policies affect the costs of adjustment.

Table I-1. Characteristics of the sample countries before adjustment

	Chile (82-83)	Côte d'Ivoire (81-83)	Ecuador (82-84)	Ghana (81-83)	Indonesia (79-81)	Malaysia (80-82)	Morocco (80-82)
GDP per capita ($US)	2 135	823	1 277	390	483	1 656	840
Annual growth rate (5 previous years)	4.2	6.6	9.0	-0.2	7.7	7.7	4.2
Share of GDP (%)							
Agriculture	8.4	34.0	13.6	58.2	25.3	26.2	17.0
Industry	25.0	10.6	19.6	7.2	12.7	23.9	16.9
Exports	20.3	35.0	24.0	7.1	30.1	55.2	19.7
Imports	26.7	38.5	23.5	7.7	22.3	54.0	33.5
Investment	20.9	28.6	24.7	5.2	27.1	31.7	22.8
Domestic savings	14.5	25.1	25.2	4.8	35.0	32.9	9.0
Budget deficit	-4.1	9.6	2.6	5.8	2.1	8.4	11.9
Share of exports (%)							
Current account deficit	47.4	50.7	34.2	8.5	-5.8	5.3	75.0
Total debt	177.6	146.6	201.4	103.5	91.6	46.2	419.1
Of which: public debt	84.1	135.9	151.8	102.6	75.0	35.6	410.3
Inflation (3 previous years) (%)	28.3	7.4	16.5	53.3	25.6	6.6	10.2
Variation (%) during the crisis of:							
Trade balance	-16.9	-24.5	-2.0	-19.0	-2.5	-14.0	-7.5
GDP	-17.2	3.5	1.0	-5.7	3.8	6.0	1.7
Debt/exports	43.3	20.8	25.5	5.3	7.9	6.3	27.2

Source: Calculations based on *World Tables*, World Bank.

Chapter II

Employment and Incomes During Adjustment

In the media, adjustment is often linked with two unfortunate effects: a growth of unemployment and a fall in wages. In reality, a more serious analysis reveals the ambiguity of the two phenomena. First, an increase in unemployment does not have the same significance as in a developed country. Consider two Third World countries, one very poor without unemployment benefits or public assistance but where one can migrate, the other a middle-income country with public benefits where it is not possible to migrate. A given number of lay-offs in the modern sector will increase unemployment much less in the first than in the second. It is actually more difficult to be unemployed — that is, to be supported by a family — in one case than the other. In the poorer country, the negative impact of adjustment will almost be hidden because lay-offs lead to expansion of the informal sector and to migration. This example shows that terms like **unemployment** and **employment** are adapted to developed economies and can lead to error if they are applied without caution to developing countries. Employment implies working full-time, and registered unemployment is linked in part to a system of unemployment benefits. These terms have little meaning in a very poor country: most economically active people are engaged in agricultural work more or less part-time, depending on the season; in towns and cities ordinarily more people are active in informal activities — where they are not employed full-time — than in the formal sector. If persons in the formal sector are laid off, unemployment does not increase as in developed countries or middle-income countries which have a system of unemployment compensation. Those who are laid off find refuge in the informal sector, which does not mean they have found new employment as this is understood in developed countries. When inappropriate terms are used, there is a possibility of misunderstanding the effects of adjustment on employment.

It is equally necessary to interpret a decline in wages. In a poor country persons employed in the modern sector could be in the top four deciles, while the lowest four deciles are composed of rural people (each decile contains 10 per cent of the population, classed by income in increasing order). In this case, if an adjustment leads to wage cuts but results in increased agricultural incomes (for example, following a devaluation which augments the prices of exported agricultural products), income inequity and poverty will decrease, although the fall in wages might lead one to think that the adjustment has socially negative effects.

These examples show that the effects of adjustment on employment and incomes can be understood only with an overall perspective. We intentionally use the term **adjustment** since structural adjustment measures sometimes play a role even if the stabilization programme is the determinant variable because of its direct effects (reducing employment and/or pay in the public sector) or the indirect effects of a fall in economic activity.

It is incorrect to think that adjustment has a simple correspondence with employment and wages, that changes in the levels of these variables depend uniquely on adjustment measures. It is impossible to explain the changes so simply because the impact of adjustment combines with other effects such as long-term demographic trends, migratory flows and the financial crisis which preceded the adjustment. The impact of adjustment alone, other things being equal, can be approximated only with a model (see

Chapter IV). That is why this chapter is entitled "Employment and Incomes During Adjustment", for it cannot pretend to evaluate the effects of adjustment alone, even though there is an effort to clarify the role of different factors, and in particular that of the adjustment measures.

1. Employment and Unemployment During an Adjustment Period

In view of the considerations mentioned above and the lack of a homogeneous labour market in developing countries, it is first necessary to distinguish between the agricultural and the non-agricultural sectors, indeed certain adjustment measures have opposite effects on the two sectors. In addition, it is necessary to take into account informal activities specific to the second sector. These activities increase because of the disequilibrium between the labour supply, which grows very rapidly in cities (5 to 6 per cent a year) and the formal sector's demand for labour, which ordinarily grows less rapidly. This disequilibrium increases and the informal sector grows to absorb surplus labour during the stagnation which results from a stabilization programme. Since demand does not follow this increase in goods and services, adjustment occurs by a fall in prices and thus in the average income of persons considered active in the informal sector. Thus in studying changes in employment three sectors should be distinguished:

— agricultural,

— informal non-agricultural,

— formal non-agricultural (public and private).

In the last, it is sometimes useful to separate public and private when their movements are known to diverge, as in Côte d'Ivoire.

Unfortunately, we do not have a detailed analysis by sector for all the countries studied, so we will give precedence to the countries for which the statistics permit such an analysis. Before examining changes in employment during the adjustment period, we must recall the effects of the crisis which usually precedes the stabilization programme.

In Chile, the 1982 crisis was accompanied by a striking decline in employment: it fell by 12 per cent and the rate of unemployment (including the beneficiaries of public works programmes) increased from 15 per cent in 1981 to 26 per cent in 1982. The drop in employment corresponds to the 14 per cent fall in the GDP. Likewise, the economic decline in Ghana during the 1970s led to a large increase in unemployment: the rate more than doubled from 1970 to 1980 in the cities, where it reached 30 per cent for men 20 to 45 years old. As we saw above, however, these two countries were exceptional compared to the other countries studied, where there had been no significant rise in unemployment before the stabilization programme. The data for the other countries in fact indicate a rise in employment or, at worst, stagnation as in Côte d'Ivoire's formal sector in 1980.

Trends in urban areas

Though employment ordinarily increased satisfactorily in the cities before the adjustment, the situation deteriorated during the adjustment period: there was a fall in employment in the formal sector, which resulted in an increase in unemployment and a swelling of the informal sector. Since there may have been other factors at work, however, these changes should not be strictly linked to the stabilization measures.

In Morocco, the population of working age (15-64 years old) in urban areas grew 5.5 per cent a year from 1982 to 1986; this growth slowed only in 1983, as migration from rural areas stopped completely after the stabilization programme was put into effect. This phenomenon is easily explained, for information on the possibilities of finding work circulates rapidly in the villages. In the same four years, the economically active urban population grew almost as fast, by 21.5 per cent as compared to 23.5 per cent, a difference resulting from the increase in schooling after age 15. During this period, employment (formal and informal sectors) grew by 16.7 per cent (the term "employment" being used for the informal sector with all the limits indicated). Thus despite the adjustment there was no fall in employment, but only a slowing of its growth, from 5.6 per cent a year between 1980 and 1982 to a still fairly rapid increase of 3.8 per cent a year. The pressure of supply increased the disequilibrium, however, resulting in a 50 per cent increase in the number of unemployed and an increase in the rate of unemployment from 12.2 to 15.6 per cent. Furthermore, the growth of the informal sector resulted from a labour surplus and not from increased growth of demand: employment in services (apart from commerce) increased by 57 per cent (compared to an 18.5 per cent increase in the growth of services nationally) while the productivity of this labour declined. The growth of employment in the non-agricultural sector was the result of divergent trends: large drops in construction and public works and in transportation, a small drop in industry and a large increase in services, the last resulting from a swelling of informal activities and the creation of jobs in the administration. These changes over the four years involved two distinct phases. From 1982 to 1984, employment in the cities stagnated and unemployment shot up by 60 per cent. From 1984 to 1986, there was renewed growth of employment and a small decline in the number of unemployed. Furthermore, in 1985 and 1986 agriculture benefited from exceptional meteorological conditions, which slowed rural migration and the growth of the labour supply in the cities. Thus it is clear that the stabilization measures of 1983 and 1984 and the economic stagnation were responsible for the large increase in unemployment and a swelling of the informal sector.

In Côte d'Ivoire, unemployment and production trends proved more unfavourable than in Morocco. Employment in the formal private sector declined regularly from 1980 to 1985, the index falling from 100 to 64.4. The losses in industry were to limited to about 10 per cent, but they attained 50 per cent in non-tradable goods and services (the construction-public works and service sectors). The fall in construction and public works was striking: the number of employees in 1985 was only 15 per cent of the 1980 level, and this fall began right at the onset of the stabilization programme (down one-third in 1981). Of course, production of enterprises in the sector also fell — by 16 per cent from 1980 to 1982, followed by a small increase of 3 per cent from 1982 to 1985 — but the fall in employment was much greater and, significantly, it continued from 1982 to 1985 despite a pick-up in production. This development was linked to stability of real wages: when demand fell, the enterprises resorted to mass lay-offs but did not reduce real wages. This stability was the result of a bias in which all categories of labour were not affected equally by the lay-offs, the hardest hit being the unskilled and youth. Thereafter, wages could fall a little whereas the average level remained constant because those who lost their jobs had been the least well paid. The opposite occurred in the public sector, with real wages declining and the number of personnel increasing regularly until 1984. The first structural adjustment measures limiting new recruitment date back to 1983 and 1984, but their effect on public employment was not felt until 1985 when there was a drop of 4.4 per cent.

A 7.7 per cent annual growth in urban labour supply from 1980 to 1985 and a 20 per cent fall in demand for labour by the modern sector (public and private) led to the usual result: a rapid increase in unemployment and a swelling of the informal sector. If the informal sector had not served as a refuge, if it had not "created" employment, the number of unemployed would have tripled and the unemployment rate would have been 42 per cent rather than 29 per cent. Conditions had been aggravated by the drought of 1983, which had spurred migration from rural areas. Furthermore, there were a large number of immigrants, especially from Burkina Faso, whose numbers continued to increase despite the poor economic conditions. These factors explain why the labour supply in the cities grew at a much higher rate than in Morocco.

Similar developments can be observed in the two Latin American countries. In Ecuador, the labour supply in cities grew 4.5 to 5 per cent annually, but before 1983 labour demand grew at the same rate, so that urban unemployment remained stable and relatively low at 6 per cent. Beginning in 1983, growth of employment slowed: for example, industrial employment grew 1.7 per cent a year from 1982 to 1986, after having increased by 9.1 per cent a year between 1975 and 1980. As a result, the unemployment rate in cities increased rapidly, reaching 12 per cent in 1986. Furthermore, part of the surplus labour found refuge in the informal sector. A 1987 survey in Quito and two other cities found that the number of underemployed in the informal sector was greater than the number of unemployed in Quito and twice the number of unemployed in the other cities. The information on Chile is less detailed since it concerns the whole country, but this drawback is attenuated by the fact that the weight of agricultural employment there is much less than in the other countries. After falling in 1982, employment dropped by another 3 per cent in 1983 but grew rapidly beginning in 1984, so that the rate of unemployment, which was 35 per cent in 1983, had dropped below its pre-crisis level by 1987. Nonetheless, the social cost of adjustment was significant since the unemployment rate was greater than 22 per cent for four years. The rates were much higher than in the other countries, but they should be understood in their context. Since Chile had a system of benefits received by between a third and a half of the unemployed, the growing disequilibrium between labour supply and demand was expressed more by a rise in unemployment than by growth of informal employment.

It appears that Indonesia also experienced this deterioration of the labour market in the non-agricultural sector. We have data on the number employed but not on the labour supply. The rate of growth of employment fell from 6.4 per cent a year in 1980-82 to 2.7 per cent a year from 1982 to 1985, a level lower than the growth of the economically active population in the cities.

Trends in rural areas

This negative assessment of the non-agricultural sector contrasts with positive trends in the agricultural sector. In Indonesia, employment grew at the same rate as the economically active population in rural areas, while labour productivity increased. Admittedly, the mechanisation of some tasks in rice cultivation reduced the need for labour, but handicraft and small business activity grew rapidly at the same time, thanks to the prosperity of agriculture. In these conditions, according to a survey of 13 villages, it appears that employment did not deteriorate during the adjustment period. Similarly, in Morocco, where the economically active male population increased by 11.4 per cent between 1982 and 1986, a 13 per cent rise in employment was accompanied by an increase in agricultural output per worker. It is certain that unemployment did not increase, and it is even possible that it fell, as indicated by a survey of the economically active rural population in 1986. This positive trend in rural employment was quite uneven from sector to sector: sharp rises in commerce and agriculture, a small decline in industry and a sharp drop in construction and public works. Owing to the relative sectoral weights, however, agriculture determined the trend in the whole rural area. This trend is explained by the growth of production as a result of good climate and certain adjustment measures (devaluation, raising of agricultural prices and liberalisation of markets). On the other hand, the fall in construction and public works was clearly a result of cuts in investment expenditure. For Côte d'Ivoire and Ghana we do not have the statistics needed to evaluate trends in rural areas. One can assume, however, that the situation was stable or declined only slightly in the former country since agricultural employment increased by 1 per cent a year, while in Ghana the situation improved as a result of large increases in production of cocoa and food crops. Moreover, since immigrant workers were a significant part of the rural work-force in Côte d'Ivoire, slow growth of employment would not necessarily increase unemployment since the adjustment could be made by reduction of immigrant labour.

These diverse and, unfortunately, uneven data nonetheless lead one to conclude that though adjustment policy often causes a sharp rise in unemployment in cities, there are two reasons why, in general, it does not have a negative effect on rural employment. First, its impact on agriculture is favourable or at least neutral, so that it does not reduce this sector's demand for labour. Second, the labour supply grows more slowly in rural areas than in cities and the conditions of employment are different. The major problem is underemployment of agricultural labour, which is linked to structural problems that are not affected by adjustment, given the growth of agricultural production in most of the cases.

2. Wages and Enterprise Incomes during the Adjustment Period

Attention is ordinarily focused on the evolution of wages, but it is preferable to consider all primary incomes to obtain a more balanced picture. In the agricultural and informal non-agricultural sectors, which account for more than half of the economically active population, most incomes are individual incomes of farmers, artisans and tradespeople, even if there are some employees. Trends in these incomes merit attention all the more since many are in the nation's low-income brackets. It is difficult to make an assessment because we do not have sufficient information on these incomes, and unbalanced information ordinarily leads to biased judgements.

The evolution of wages

We first try to assess changes in wages and profits in the formal non-agricultural sector, knowing that the scope of the assessment varies with the sector's weight in each country, from a small minority of the economically active population in Côte d'Ivoire and Ghana to a majority in Chile. One should distinguish between government and private employees because their wages can follow different trends and can even move in opposite directions, as in Côte d'Ivoire. This has a simple explanation: the pay of public employees depends entirely on the government, and stabilization measures frequently entail its reduction. On the other hand, a government can only influence private sector pay — for example, by setting minimum wages. Stabilization programmes often entail sharp cuts in the purchasing power of public employees. For example, in Chile average real wages fell by 19.5 per cent in 1983 from its 1982 level, and the trend continued until 1985, when it was 24 per cent lower. Similarly, there was a fall of 16 per cent in Côte d'Ivoire from 1981 to 1984 and of 13 per cent in Morocco from 1982 to 1985. Nonetheless, this decline is not inevitable: in Indonesia public employees retained their purchasing power, while in Ghana it was increased. The latter country is a quite special case, however, for the pay of public employees had been cut back so drastically before the adjustment that even after the increase it was only half the level at the end of the 1970s. Given the income brackets of public employees, cuts in the public payroll, in principle, do not affect the lowest deciles and thus do not increase poverty. This conclusion must be qualified, for some public employees must support extended families, as in Côte d'Ivoire. This means that income per capita would be low in these families supported by an employee with an income near the average of the active population. This family burden is the result of the relatively privileged situation of public employees before the adjustment, which obliged them to welcome numerous relatives. When their pay was cut drastically, the burden could not be shed and the family risked falling below the poverty line.

Contrary to what may be assumed, real wages (nominal wages deflated by the consumer price index) in the private sector do not necessarily fall during an adjustment period. Of course, wages fell in the two Latin American countries. In industry, the decline between 1982 and 1985 reached 19 per cent in Ecuador and 24 per cent in Chile. In the latter country, there was an even greater fall of 46 per cent in the construction sector, the one most affected by stabilization. A study based on a large sample of Chilean enterprises covering all sectors and regions indicated an average fall of 27 per cent during the period, which is consistent with the preceding figures by sector. Morocco also saw a fall in real wages, but it was smaller: 13 per cent in industry from 1983 to 1986. This was the prolongation of a trend observed before the stabilization programme, since average wages had fallen by 6.3 per cent between 1980 and 1983.

Apparently there was no fall in Côte d'Ivoire, Indonesia and Malaysia. In Côte d'Ivoire, private enterprises reduced their payrolls by extensive lay-offs and the average wage remained stable. In reality, the lay-offs hit low-skilled labour more than skilled labour, so our estimate of average pay is biased. This stability was due in part to a skill effect, for the composition of labour changed from 1980 to 1985. In the Asian countries, however, there was a clear improvement. Real wages in Indonesia increased by 7 per cent in industry and 4 per cent in the tertiary sector between 1982 and 1985. Average wages rose in Malaysia by 6 per cent a year in 1985 and 1986. Admittedly, from 1987 the effects of the stabilization programme were felt on the labour market: there was a small decline in real wages. Nevertheless, the balance remained positive with an increase of 9 per cent from 1984 to 1987. The performance of the Asian countries was thus contrary to the experience of the Latin American cases.

It is useful to round off these data with a comment on the minimum wage, when there is one. Though this wage is usually not respected in the agricultural and informal sectors, it is ordinarily respected by private enterprises of the formal sector. Changes in the minimum wage apply to low-income urban workers. In Chile and Ecuador, it moved in parallel with the average wages mentioned above. Côte d'Ivoire reduced it 8 per cent by not adjusting for inflation, whereas many enterprises adjusted wages to the cost of living. On the other hand, the minimum wage was increased by 1 per cent a year in Morocco during the adjustment period. That explains the stability of the average wage in industry, which primarily employs labour with minimal skills and paid the minimum wage. A comparison between these countries is interesting. Of course, variations in the average wage depend on supply and demand in the formal sector labour market, and hence on changes in demand related to the economic situation, which was quite unfavourable in Chile and Ecuador, and less so in Indonesia and Malaysia. However, a government's minimum-wage policy can significantly moderate the impact of an unfavourable situation, as the Moroccan example shows.

The evolution of profits

Estimating incomes of enterprises in the formal sector is much more difficult; at best one can indicate the trends. The first question is the wage-profit division. Does stabilization reduce wages and profits simultaneously, so that their ratio does not change, or is the cost of stabilization borne by the wage-earner? In Chile the share of wages in the national income was 36 per cent in 1980 and 42 per cent in 1981; it remained at 42.5 per cent for 1984 to 1986. To be sure, this indicator is not as appropriate as the share of wages in value added; but this finding suggests that the share of wages in value added has not declined. P. Meller concludes from this the cost of adjustment was mainly borne by workers laid off, while those who retained their employment, despite a decline in wages, did not bear a greater cost than owners of enterprises.

On the other hand, in Ecuador the share of wages in value added clearly declined in industry; this finding is consistent with the downward trend in wages and the stability of labour productivity. The trend appeared equally favourable to profits in Morocco, where from 1981 to 1985 the share of wages in value added of industry declined from 43 to 41 per cent. However, in industries that make intensive use of labour with minimal skills (textiles, clothing and leather) the trend was the opposite, owing to the revaluation of the legal minimum wage. A survey in a limited sample of 40 enterprises affected by the liberalisation of foreign trade revealed diverse situations: in a majority of cases profits increased as a result of a growth of sales, but a minority of enterprises did less well as a result of increased financing costs and a drop in sales caused by foreign competition; the latter had to support higher amortization costs while working at 40 per cent of capacity. We do not have data on construction enterprises, but it is certain that they suffered from the cuts in investment expenditure. The Moroccan example reveals the diversity in sectoral trends: an overall increase in profits is compatible with sectoral losses associated with adjustment measures. In Côte d'Ivoire, the income share of profits clearly increased between 1980 and 1985 in modern sector enterprises affiliated with the Centrale des Bilans, except for services. Malaysia provides the only counter-example: the income share of profits fell during the adjustment period because wages increased more than the productivity of labour.

Except in Malaysia, it appears that profits were less affected than wages by stabilization programmes. The situation is ordinarily the contrary in developed countries, where profits fall more than wages during a recession. This difference stems from a dualism of the labour market in developing countries, where the informal sector represents a labour reserve which makes it easier to cut real wages during a recession. This favourable picture for profits must be qualified, however, for some enterprises are hit hard and forced into bankruptcy by measures such as cuts in public investment, increases in interest rates and deregulation of foreign trade. Thus an adjustment period is highly discriminating for entrepreneurs: some, often a majority, see their profits rise, while others suffer losses of income or go out of business.

The evolution of the informal sector

Our knowledge of income trends in the informal sector is very limited because of the nature of this sector. At best, we can make some hypotheses. When unemployment rises rapidly in urban areas, which as we have seen occurs during an adjustment period, there is a simultaneous increase in the number of persons working in the informal sector, which serves as a refuge for the unemployed who cannot be supported by their families, an indispensable support because there are no unemployment benefits, except in the case of Chile. Now, the informal sector's output depends on the number of persons active in it, given the unimportant role of capital. Consequently, this increase in persons active and in supply, when the stabilization programme reduces demand, results in lower prices and incomes in the informal sector. This was observed in urban areas of Ecuador, where the income of the economically active population with low educational levels, most of whom work in the informal sector, fell by 20 per cent between 1982 and 1987. Ghana can also be mentioned, even if it is a special case, for the increased state control of the modern sector resulted in rapid growth of the informal sector during the 1970s. The 1983 programme had the effect of suddenly cutting commercial margins and, consequently, the incomes of small vendors, who are usually women, reducing this overdeveloped sector in favour of directly productive activities. Our knowledge of the situation in Côte d'Ivoire and Morocco is more tenuous since it is based on simulations of a macro-micro model (see Chapter IV) which reproduces the observed developments. According to the model, average income in Morocco dropped sharply (more than 10 per cent) between 1982 and 1985 before attaining its previous level in 1986 as a result of the recovery (GDP increase of 8.4 per cent); average income also fell in Côte d'Ivoire after 1981. In every case, then, average income in the informal sector drops during the adjustment period, and this has negative social consequences because the majority of persons working in the informal sector are in the low-income working population in cities.

Changes in agriculture

Trends in agricultural sector incomes seem generally less negative, for several reasons. First, some adjustment measures have a positive impact, while those with negative effects, such as wage reductions for public employees, do not hit agriculture directly. Devaluation has the most positive impact because it increases prices of tradable goods in relation to non-tradable goods and benefits agricultural exports. In some countries, like Morocco, Côte d'Ivoire and Ghana, the governments greatly increased the producer prices of agricultural products after carrying out a devaluation and reducing government levies. Some public monopolies have been ended, like those for selling seeds and fertilizer in Morocco, and for processing and marketing rice in Côte d'Ivoire. Of course, other adjustment measures — like the cutting of fertilizer subsidies in Indonesia which slowed the growth of rice production — have reduced agricultural incomes. The same step in Ghana may have reduced the incomes of food crop producers. On the whole, however, adjustment measures have contributed to higher agricultural incomes. On the other hand, exogenous factors like the weather or international market prices sometimes have had a determining effect on agricultural incomes during an adjustment period, relegating the adjustment measures to a secondary role. Morocco's exceptional drought of 1981, the same country's good rainfall in 1985-86 and Côte d'Ivoire's drought of 1983 had a greater impact on agricultural incomes than did macroeconomic and agricultural policies. International prices also have a considerable impact, which can be temporarily fended off only by stabilization funds guaranteeing a price higher than that of the international market, as in Côte d'Ivoire. In that country, the 1987 fall in world coffee prices was translated into lower producer prices only in 1990. The 1982-83 crisis in Malaysia was due to falling prices for oil and tin as well as for rubber and palm oil, which fell 2 and 28 per cent respectively from 1981 to 1982. With the exception of Côte d'Ivoire in 1983, however, these exogenous factors did not cause a sharp drop of agricultural incomes during the three or four years after a stabilization programme was put into effect. This combination of circumstances and the positive effects of adjustment measures explain the satisfactory trend in agricultural incomes during the adjustment period.

A comparison of non-food monetary expenditure by farmers in Côte d'Ivoire, based on surveys in 1979 and 1985, reveals a clear per capita increase of 11 to 27 per cent. There was a smaller rise in incomes of about 1 per cent per annum for persons producing the main crops. Nonetheless, the trend is upward, and it has been shown that peasants' incomes did not decrease during the adjustment period. Incomes of cocoa planters in Ghana benefited from a sharp rise in real prices and a one-third increase in output. There was also an improvement in Morocco, where the output of small farmers, mainly growing cereals and legumes, increased by an average of 40 per cent in 1984 and 1985 without any fall in real prices of these products. The medium and large farmers benefited from rapid growth in output of cereals, citrus fruits and early fruits and vegetables, and from price increases linked to devaluations. When Indonesia became self-sufficient in rice in 1984-85, the increase in its output slowed, but that marked the start of a rapid rise in output of other agricultural products. At the same time, increased mechanisation resulted in increases in productivity and incomes of persons working in agriculture during the adjustment period. During Malaysia's adjustment period, the output of persons working in agriculture continued to increase. To be sure, some persons such as rubber planters lost income in 1984, but others such as producers of palm oil gained and in any case these trends due to shifts in international prices rather than to stabilization policies. From 1984 to 1987, there was also a rise in incomes of rice growers, the main low-income group, as a result of government infrastructural investment during the 1970s.

The only case in which peasant incomes fell was in Ecuador, but this was not due to a drop in agricultural incomes. Actually, the greater part of the income of small farmers comes from the non-agricultural sector because their holdings are too small for subsistence. They have to work in the non-agricultural sector and especially suffered from the fall in wages. In addition, only large farmers produce for export. Consequently, incomes of small farmers fell by about 20 per cent between 1982 and 1987 because of the recession in the non-agricultural sector. In contrast, the real incomes of large farmers remained almost the same as a result of the devaluations.

This picture, including the special case of small Ecuadorian farmers, points to two conclusions. The incomes of persons working in agriculture were maintained or increased during the adjustment period. The fact that some adjustment measures are favourable to agriculture contributed to this, but exogenous factors were at least as important.

This picture will be rounded off by some observations on the wages of agricultural workers. They were only a small minority in the countries studied, but their conditions deserve attention since they are among the poorest of the working population. In some cases, changes in their incomes paralleled those of farmers. For example, in Java real wages in agriculture increased 12 per cent between 1983 and 1986, the situation being favourable to workers since there was a labour shortage during seasonal peaks in rice cultivation. This shortage results from a development of non-agricultural activities in villages and small cities, which increases employment possibilities in rural areas. The average wage on Malaysian rubber plantations was raised in 1985, but in 1984 it was the same as in 1982-83, while there had been a small increase in the average wage on palm oil plantations in 1984. This resistance to wage cuts, despite the circumstances of stabilization, is in part explained by the structure of the agricultural labour market: workers on rubber plantations are the most unionised of the Malaysian economy, and they have obtained partial indexation of their wages. The only available data for Morocco concern the legal minimum wage, which increased 10 per cent between 1983 and 1986. Of course, this is widely disregarded in rural areas, but it appears probable that real wages did not fall during the adjustment period because of trends in the agricultural labour market: falling unemployment and a need for labour as a result of a large increase in output of large farms. The picture was different in Côte d'Ivoire, where the legal minimum wage in 1982-83 was 8 per cent less than in 1979-80, and where immigrant workers make up a large part of the labour supply in rural areas. Given the pressure of this excess labour, it is possible that real wages in agriculture fell after 1981. Agricultural workers suffered greatly from the recession in Ecuador, where the legal minimum wage fell by 15 per cent between 1982 and 1985, and where data on the wage bill would indicate at least an equivalent fall in real wages. This clearly contrasts with employers, namely the large farmers, whose incomes remained almost unchanged. This can be explained by the fall in the average income of the small farmers. Since some of the latter looked for work as labourers, large farmers took advantage of the excess labour supply to reduce wages. This analysis of agricultural wages shows that they are linked to the general situation in agriculture: the evolution of output, employment and prices. The cases studied show that incomes of agricultural workers ordinarily move in parallel to those of small peasants.

Chapter III

Living Standards and Poverty During Adjustment

To study a population's living standards, and in particular those of the poor, it is necessary to know the changes in primary incomes, as described in Chapter II, because the living standards of households largely depend on their primary incomes. They also depend on free state services, government transfers (e.g. subsidies on goods and aid to persons), and private transfers (e.g. remittances of emigrant workers). Some adjustment measures directly or indirectly affect these services and transfers and thus have an impact on living standards of households. For example, budget cuts can reduce educational services or food subsidies, while a devaluation can increase remittances. These transfers also depend on other factors, however: economic conditions in a country where emigrants work, or political measures concerning the emigrants, can greatly reduce their remittances. As in Chapter II, the developments described here resulted from adjustment measures and numerous other internal or external factors.

A family's living standard corresponds to its total net income (in money and kind) divided by the number of members. This income thus encompasses primary incomes (including self-consumption), less direct taxes, plus services and transfers provided by the state and private transfers, that is to say, primary incomes and net secondary incomes. The family structure can introduce another factor. For example, in developed countries it is observed that a rapid increase in single-parent families, other things being equal, leads to an increase in poverty. Actually, this involves families headed by women who, having children to support, find it difficult to work. Consequently, the income per member in such families is very low. Since this sort of abrupt change is much less common in developing countries and since the periods studied are brief (four or five years), it is assumed here that the family structure did not change. Though this hypothesis appears realistic, another is questionable. Since our information on primary incomes is based on economic groups, we have assumed that all working family members were employed in the same group: for example, if the head of the family had a small farm, we assume the other working family members work on this farm, so that the primary incomes of the family simply changed with the average income of the group. This assumption simplifies reality, for in cities one family member can work in the informal sector while the head of family is employed in the modern sector. In such cases, there can be compensatory phenomena between the loss of one and the gain of the other, which are not taken into account here.

Using this simplified approach, we will trace the evolution of secondary incomes before trying to assess trends in the living standards of different groups.

1. Living Standards and Social Indicators

Secondary incomes and living standards

In an adjustment period, subsidies are of primordial importance because of their political repercussions. The most familiar image derived from the media is that of revolts against stabilization programmes because they eliminate food subsidies. In fact, the problem of subsidies is more complex than

41

it may appear. Even food subsidies may mainly benefit households which are not among the poor, and there are subsidies which benefit only rich households, as shown by the example of Chilean subsidies for debtors owing dollars.

The problem of food subsidies was the most serious in Morocco. In June 1981, 50 per cent price increases on primary products led to riots in Casablanca, which caused dozens of deaths and hundreds of wounded and forced the government to withdraw the stabilization programme. Additional riots caused many casualties in January 1984, following two waves of price hikes in August 1983 and January 1984. As a result, the government had to give up reducing the subsidies on everyday products. It was possible to stabilize prices at a lower cost because of the fall in prices on the international market (95 per cent of the subsidised food oil, 80 per cent of the subsidised soft wheat and 50 per cent of the subsidised sugar were imported in 1985). The only austerity measure retained was the ending of subsidies on intermediate products (butter, milk and quality soft wheat). Despite this measure and the fall in international prices, the cost of subsidies increased during adjustment from 1.5 billion dirhams in 1982 to 2.8 billion dirhams in 1985, which represented a significant share of the government's current expenditure (11.6 per cent). In constant prices, the per capita cost of subsidies did not change from 1982 to 1985. Owing to the risk of serious political reactions, then, the government did not reduce the subsidies despite the budget cuts of the stabilization programme.

An analysis of the impact of these subsidies on household living standards reveals their ambiguity. On the one hand, they provide few benefits to the poor, for the households in the three lowest deciles received only 16 per cent of them, on the other they were indispensable for their survival: in cities, the food consumption of the poor would be cut by one-fourth if the subsidies were abolished. This is a specifically urban problem, for in rural areas the poor more often live on a subsistence basis, and thus the subsidies represent less than 5 per cent of their total consumption, compared with 20 per cent in the cities. This leads to a paradoxical situation in which, to guarantee the minimum food necessities for the urban poor, the state finances a transfer in which 47 per cent of the benefits accrue to the comfortable households in deciles 8, 9 and 10. If the subsidised goods are produced locally, this policy also has an impact on the average income of farmers: it should increase the income of producers by stimulating consumption and hence demand.

The state also provides direct aid to poor families — food supplements for mothers, meals in school canteens and employment at public work sites in rural areas — in an amount equivalent to the food subsidies they receive. These transfers were not affected by the stabilization programme: the number of pupils receiving free meals increased from 570 000 in 1984 to 663 000 in 1986. Furthermore, the wages at public work sites followed the cost of living since they corresponded to the minimum legal wage.

The successive stabilization programmes in Côte d'Ivoire reduced subsidies and increased charges for services so that the state would no longer be financing the deficits of state enterprises. Thus rail, bus and air fares, were raised, along with water and electricity rates. Subsidies on rice as well as on housing for public employees were reduced. The impact of these truth-in-pricing measures depends on whether the share of the good concerned in household expenses increases or decreases with household income. The housing and air transport subsidies benefited only well-to-do households. By contrast, the proportion of the household budget devoted to water and electricity decreases as the income increases[1]. Thus the reductions in those subsidies had a relatively greater affect on poor households than on others.

Adjustment in Ghana brought about an efficacious restructuring of subsidies. Under a policy of compensations which had evolved in the 1970s, the modern sector and public employees accepted low wages because the state kept food prices low with subsidies. The penury of goods on the official market, however, led public employees to sell part of these goods on the black market. The adjustment policies completely changed this system, abolishing subsidies, but in compensation establishing several programmes of food aid targeted at the poorest groups (free school meals, furnishing medicines and providing work for the unemployed in the north, with remuneration in food). Such a reform had an obvious redistributive effect since it subsidised consumption by the more disadvantaged persons rather than by employees of the modern sector.

Chile provides a textbook case on subsidies: and actually had the peculiarity of having increased government aid to the richest and the poorest groups at the same time. In 1982, about half of the domestic loans were denominated in dollars, the other half in pesos. After the devaluations of 1982, however, the Central Bank compensated the losses of the dollar debtors by providing them with a preferential rate of exchange so that they could reimburse their debts throughout the adjustment period at the rate that had prevailed prior to the devaluation. This subsidy cost an average of 4 per cent of GDP from 1983 to 1985, a large sum. Furthermore, at the time of the 24 per cent devaluation in September 1984, debtors owing dollars were permitted to convert these debts into pesos at the pre-devaluation exchange rate, which represented a subsidy of $230 million, or 1.5 per cent of GDP. The pesos debtors also received subsidies in the form of special loans at subsidised interest rates, seven points lower than market rates, and debt rescheduling that gave one year interest-free. We do not have information on the distribution of these subsidies by income group, but it is certain that the high-income groups were the main beneficiaries. They were the ones who had the easiest access to dollar loans.

Moreover, during the adjustment period Chile carried out a policy of aiding the poor whose efficacy was incontestable. While government social expenditure was decreased, there was an increase in subsidies for very disadvantaged households (the 10 or 15 per cent poorest). This programme consisted of distributing food to pregnant woman and to children less than six years old, and providing free meals for children in primary schools. The food was distributed in health centres where the pregnant woman and child could be examined and the food ration could be increased in cases of malnutrition. As a result of this programme infant mortality and malnutrition among children decreased during the adjustment period, and Chile's rate of infant mortality became one of the lowest in Latin America.

On the other hand, households hit by unemployment suffered from a reduction of unemployment benefits. The number of unemployed almost doubled from 1981 to 1984, but unemployment benefits were cut nearly in half in real terms. In these conditions, it can be estimated that the subsidies received by the poorest (1st decile) and the richest (10th decile) increased during the adjustment period, while those received by the poor (2nd and 3rd deciles) decreased.

The neo-liberal programme of Ecuador's President Cordero, elected in 1984, entailed a reduction of subsidies on agricultural inputs and certain agricultural products, although Cordero represented the interests of agricultural exporters. To be sure, this reduction was compensated by an exchange rate very favourable to agricultural exports. After economic difficulties had created wide discontent, however, Cordero reinstated subsidies, contrary to his principles, by financing public works programmes in rural areas, especially in the coastal region which was his electoral base. This policy, based on electoral considerations, resulted in renewed inflation and a return to budget deficits. This example shows the political character of subsidies, whatever the government's doctrine or ideology.

Expenditure on education and health customarily accounts for most social expenditure. Its evolution in an adjustment period is of cardinal importance since poor and sometimes middle-income households cannot compensate for cuts in these government services by going to the private sector. Cuts in health services have immediate effects on their living standards, and there are also long-term consequences: children deprived of schooling and proper health care will be less productive in 20 or 30 years and will thus have a lower income, thereby trapping these families in a vicious circle of poverty from one generation to another. It is necessary to distinguish between expenditure and services, however, for the stabilization measures involve expenditure, while family living standards depend on services. To give a simple example, consider the case of elementary schooling: to decrease expenditure by 10 per cent, a government could cut wages by 13 per cent (assuming the payroll represented 80 per cent of the total expenditure on that item). In this case, the families would receive the same services as before the adjustment. This reasoning could be misleading, however, for if a government repeats this step several times it will undermine the quality of education, but this negative effect can be avoided if such a step is taken only once. The risk is less obvious in certain countries in which, for historic reasons (colonial status), the pay of teachers was very high to begin with.

Morocco provides a good illustration of this distinction. In budgetary terms, adjustment entailed incontestable social costs, with social expenditure dropping from 8.3 per cent of GDP in 1983 to 7.2 per cent in 1986. During that period, per capita expenditure fell for education by 11 per cent and for health by 5 per cent. It cannot be said that social expenditures were sacrificed in budget terms since their share of the budget did not fall, but per capita social expenditure fell sharply because of rapid population growth, even though the stabilization measures had only slightly reduced government expenditure.

Nonetheless, the educational and health services received by families were not reduced on the whole. The number of secondary school pupils increased 22 per cent between 1983 and 1986, and those in higher education by 29 per cent, with an improved balance for girls (+54 per cent). By contrast, primary school enrolments fell by 10 per cent, but this drop cannot be attributed to a decline in educational services. Actually, the number of teachers increased by 14 per cent and the number of pupils per class clearly decreased. There was a fall in demand — especially in rural areas, where the decline in pupils was greater than in cities — that was probably due to adjustment: in a period of stagnation and lay-offs by the modern sector, poor families give up sending their children to school to avoid certain costs and because schooling appears to have no purpose when it no longer leads to employment in the modern sector.

In sum, if one weights the number enroled by the unit costs, it is clear that per capita educational services did not diminish despite the budget cuts. This paradox is explained by the wage policy. Real pay of teachers fell by 18 per cent on average from 1983 to 1986. Furthermore, expenditure on equipment was reduced sharply. This measure and the wage policy would certainly have affected the quality of education if the stabilization programme had continued for more than three or four years. In other respects, educational social services were not touched. For example, grant is essential for a child from a poor family, or fairly poor family, to attend the university; the number of grants increased by 36 per cent between 1983 and 1986 and more than half of the students have them. Thus in the short term families did not suffer from a decline in educational services or associated aid.

The example of education reveals that in certain cases there is a margin for budget cuts which permits reconciling efficiency and equity in a stabilization programme. There was a similar record in the area of health. Although the number of beds per inhabitant fell because all investment in hospitals was suspended, the number of medical examinations in public health facilities increased by 13 per cent in the cities and by 26 per cent in the rural areas from 1982 to 1987. This last figure is interesting because it mostly concerns poor families who have little or no access to private medical care. In addition, the number of medical personnel per capita increased rapidly during the adjustment as a result of the efforts put into education in the 1970s, Nevertheless, stagnation of current expenditure led to a lack of funds for the hospitals and, as a result, a deterioration of care, while the lack of new construction penalised rural residents since half of them live more than six kilometres from a medical facility.

The educational and health services of Côte d'Ivoire and Ghana were more sensitive to the conditions of adjustment, even though in some instances there was continued growth in the services provided. In Côte d'Ivoire, the 12 per cent increase in the number of elementary school pupils from 1981 to 1985 was less than that of the school-age population. There was a 22 per cent increase of pupils in secondary school, but the stabilization measures halted the growth of higher education, which in 1984 was at 1980 level. This was not necessarily a negative effect of adjustment, for the economic climate made employment prospects appear rather limited for graduates of higher education. In Ghana, from 1983 on there was only a small increase in pupils, but there was an improvement in the quality of instruction, which had greatly deteriorated because of the decline in spending per pupil during the 1970s and because the public sector wage policy had led to increasing recruitment of unqualified teachers. Furthermore, there were cuts in educational social services in the two countries. The second stabilization programme of 1984-85 in Côte d'Ivoire entailed a cut of 50 per cent in the number of grants for higher education and of 30 per cent for secondary schools. The 1987 adjustment measures in Ghana introduced payments for school textbooks and led to cuts in subsidies for canteens and lodging for many pupils.

Ghana carried out a similar policy in the domain of health, increasing the daily cost of hospitalisation and of consultations in 1985, which seemed to put a brake on demand. Actually, the number of hospital days stagnated during the adjustment period, after having dropped precipitously in 1983 when per capita public expenditure on health fell to only one-fourth of the level at the beginning of 1970s. This resulted in such a lack of medicine and qualified personnel that fewer and fewer sick persons went to the hospital.

Adjustment had greater negative consequences on social expenditures in the Latin American countries. In both cases, these expenditures were accorded smaller shares in a budget that was itself reduced. Thus in Chile their share fell from 30 per cent before adjustment to 23 per cent. Consequently, despite a low rate of population growth, per capita social expenditure fell 20 per cent between 1981 and 1983-86, whether one considers education, health or housing. This reduction hit poor families (1st to 4th deciles) more than others because these services and social security payments represent a much greater proportion of their total resources than for the other households. Although their share of personal incomes was only 12 per cent, they received 50 per cent of the health and educational expenditures and 20 per cent of the social security payments. Ecuador also reduced the share of social expenditure in the budget, with the result that educational expenditure fell from 5 to 4 per cent of GDP and health expenditure from 2 to 1.1 per cent of the GDP. This decision caused drops in per capita expenditure of 29 per cent for education and 35 per cent for health between 1980-82 and 1984-86.

The two Asian countries took the opposite course, safeguarding social expenditure so that households, especially the poor, did not suffer from a loss of services during adjustment. Social expenditure rose in Malaysia from 23 to 28 per cent of current expenditure between 1984 and 1987, while its share in investment expenditure remained nearly stable. Consequently, expenditure for education increased by 5.7 per cent a year and that for health by 3.7 per cent a year, well above the rate of population growth. Furthermore, the composition of these expenditures shifted in favour of the poor, as indicated by a comparison of the plan for capital expenditure with the actual capital outlay. Thus there was a large cut in expenditure for new hospitals, but not for rural health services. Other indicators corroborating this favourable evolution of educational and health services during adjustment were a 17 per cent increase in the number of teachers between 1984 and 1986 and an increase in the already high percentage of children attending primary school. Furthermore, there was an encouraging decline in the number of persons per doctor from 3 400 to 3 000. When Indonesia cut its public expenditure, allocations for education and health were the least affected, at least until 1986-87, when they were cut as much as other budget items. Nonetheless, social expenditure was temporarily or permanently favoured, while in Chile and Ecuador it was the first to be sacrificed.

Morocco was the only country of the sample for which private transfers from abroad were important. These remittances mounted rapidly during the period studied: their nominal value rose from 4.5 billion dirhams in 1980 to 10.6 billion in 1984 and 14.4 billion in 1987, or an increase of 80 per cent in real terms in seven years. The transfers played a decisive role in Morocco. To understand their impact, it is necessary to compare them with the expenditures of households in the first six deciles, for it is plausible that most of these remittances benefit those households. The remittances amounted to 29 per cent of their expenditures in 1980 and 37 per cent in 1985. These transfers were thus a large and growing part of household resources during the adjustment period. The main factor in this growth was the policy of the countries receiving the immigrants, especially that of France, which did not limit the employment of this immigrant labour and permitted funds to be transferred freely. Moreover, these remittances were encouraged by measures such as devaluations and special foreign currency accounts that received higher rates of interest than other accounts. In this case, macroeconomic measures had direct social consequences.

Other private transfers — internal ones in this case — play an important role in sub-Saharan Africa. For example, it was shown how each employee of the modern sector in Côte d'Ivoire, especially each public employee, is enmeshed in a web of community obligations, which involve large transfers to more or less distant relatives. These transfers often go to families living in rural areas, with no one employed in the modern sector, and thus amount to a private redistribution of income. Since these obligations are not determined by the economic situation, public employees whose pay had been greatly reduced (see Chapter II) often found themselves in difficulty: their resources available for consumption by the immediate family had been reduced more than their pay.

To determine the evolution of living standards of families, ranked by income or socio-economic group of the head of family, it would be necessary to have estimates of their available resources plus transfers in kind. Unfortunately, such information is rarely available and what exists is incomplete.

Two surveys on household consumption in both Malaysia and Indonesia, before and after adjustment, provide some interesting information on family resources but do not take into account services provided by the state. In Indonesia a large random sample of 50 000 households was surveyed in 1984 and 1987. They indicate that consumption and per capita income rose rapidly for families of peasants and agricultural workers. The picture was similar for families of persons employed in the non-agricultural sector. The evolution was also favourable for tradespeople, the largest group of independent persons in the non-agricultural sector. Since we know that educational and health expenditures were relatively protected until 1986-87, it is certain that the living standards of these families improved significantly from 1984 to 1987.

The two surveys on family incomes in Malaysia were made in the same years. They indicate that average family income fell by 5 per cent in urban areas but increased in rural areas. Some more detailed data show there were gains by small rubber planters, rice growers and agricultural workers on large plantations, but families of small coconut planters suffered a small loss of income. Owing to the evolution of social expenditure, living standards of rural families, with some exceptions, improved from 1984 to 1987, while the decline in average urban incomes was cushioned by these government transfers.

On the other hand, household living standards dropped sharply in Ecuador and Chile during the adjustment period. This is only an estimate for Ecuador: the average household income, including transfers, was calculated for each group, then this income was deflated in proportion to a consumer price index for each group, and finally the real per capita average income was calculated on the basis of the population by group. These estimates indicate that there was a fall in income, which was much greater for the small farmers than the large. Conversely, urban families with a high educational level suffered a much greater loss than families with a low educational level. Thus it can be concluded that every group suffered a sharp drop in living standards, with the exception of large farmers (a small minority), who more or less were able to maintain their standard of living. For Chile, we know only family expenditures in Santiago in 1978 and 1988. The average expenditure was unchanged, but the share of richest 20 per cent (5th quintile) had clearly grown at the expense of the other households, whose average consumption therefore fell from 1978 to 1988. In light of the reduction of social expenditure (see above), this fall was not compensated by government transfers, except for the poorest (or the 1st decile, which corresponds to the poorest 10 per cent) who benefited from targeted aid (see above). This decline began before the 1983 stabilization programme, however, for the crisis of 1982 was so serious that the fall in household living standards began that year. Moreover, this fall especially hit poor to middle-income households (2nd to 8th deciles), while the poorest households (1st decile) and the richest (9th and 10th deciles) were less affected.

The surveys on household consumption in Morocco in 1971 and 1985 were too far apart in time to shed light on trends between 1982-83 and 1985. We therefore used a macro-micro model (see Chapter IV) to get a general idea of average income by group. The incomes correspond to primary incomes plus the transfers by the emigrants. Government services, subsidies and assistance are not taken into account. In rural areas, average income for all groups increased from 1982 to 1985, a trend which was confirmed in 1986. In urban areas the results are different. To be sure, the average income of self-employed persons in the modern sector increased in 1985-86, but only after having fallen in 1984. This decline was much greater for persons working in the informal sector, but there was a recovery and the 1982 level was surpassed in 1986. By contrast, persons employed by the modern sector lost ground. If it is assumed that their families had to support the unemployed, which appears plausible, the average income of these families declined from 1982 to 1986 by 12 per cent. Although, per capita food subsidies as well as educational and health services in cities were not decreased, that could not prevent a decline in the living standards of persons employed by the modern sector. This picture should be qualified, for within this group different developments were possible. For example, the family of a skilled worker whose son becomes unemployed has suffered two losses, because of the fall in wages for skilled workers. On the other hand, there was no decline in the living standard of an unskilled worker's family which received funds from an emigrant relative.

Social indicators

The difficulties of determining living standards make a complementary approach useful. Social indicators are usually concerned with health — the rate of infant mortality, life expectancy and the level of malnutrition — but they can refer to other domains such as the percentages of children attending school, or the percentage of households having access to potable water or having a given durable good. The advantage of these indicators is that they are independent of prices and avoid all the problems involved in calculating real incomes. However, these indicators are not always available for the years that interest us (before the adjustment and three or four years afterwards), and also it is only possible to give a general idea of their variations. On the other hand, it is necessary to be aware of the unreliability of certain indicators such as infant mortality. For many developing countries the statistics on this subject must be used with caution.

The indicators for health in Morocco appear to have been favourable. For example, the rate of infant mortality declined by four points between 1983 and 1987, from 96 to 92 per 1 000. The rate of decline slowed, however, for it had been dropping by two points a year before 1983. Life expectancy continued to increase at the same rate, by 1.4 years from 1980 to 1983 and by 1.8 years from 1983 to 1987. However, these short-term variations are of limited significance because of the phenomenon of inertia. We have already seen that the percentage of secondary school attendance and university enrolment increased while that of elementary school attendance decreased. Finally, possession of consumer durables (television sets, motorbikes, sewing machines and automobiles) rapidly increased, except for automobiles.

Our information on Côte d'Ivoire and Ghana is more limited. In Ghana, the rate of infant mortality declined during the 1980s, but a 1985 survey on the weight of infants revealed that 35 per cent were less than 80 per cent of the weight considered normal in the United States. This figure had been 51 per cent in 1983 after a drought, before declining to 35 per cent in 1985. Likewise, the calorie intake stabilized in the 1980s after having fallen in the 1970s. The percentage of secondary school attendance did not change, but the percentage of children attending elementary school decreased. Even if this decline is attributable to lower demand rather than availability of schooling, it will have long-term consequences for productivity and incomes, as has been noted. Thus it can be assumed that there was no aggravation of the situation during 1983-87, it being understood that some indicators are rather mediocre because of the deterioration of living conditions in Ghana from the 1970s to 1983. The social indicators for Côte d'Ivoire were also stable on average. Percentages for school attendance did not greatly change, with a small increase at the secondary level and a small decrease at the elementary level. Increase in life expectancy and a decline in the rate of infant mortality were maintained. Finally, the per capita calorie intake did not change.

In Latin America, there is a contrast between the fall in living standards of the majority of the population and certain social indicators. In Ecuador, there was a continued increase in life expectancy and decline in the rate of infant mortality. Likewise in Chile, the rate of infant mortality and percentage of children suffering from malnutrition declined, and by the end of the 1980s Chile's rate of infant mortality was one of the lowest in Latin America. The percentages of school attendance had been high and remained stable during the 1980s. Thus the record of the social indicators is much less negative than that for living standards. This is inherent in certain indicators: the percentage of school attendance provides no information on the quality of instruction; increased use of a vaccine or other medical procedure can lower infant mortality while family incomes fall. In addition, as mentioned above, a policy targeted at the poorest can have an impact on the indicator concerned, whatever the fate of other poor families.

2. Poverty

The problem of poverty is at the heart of current debates on the consequences of adjustment. Despite the complexity of the issue, despite the number of factors involved, one simple, even simplistic, question is always raised: Has not adjustment increased poverty? An affirmative answer suggested by the misery in the poorest neighbourhoods of a capital is not a scientific response. In dealing with this subject, it is necessary to take the entire country into account, for it is possible that the living conditions of 1 million poor people in the countryside are improved although 200 000 new poor people can be counted in the capital. In addition, trends in poverty depend on many factors. Their weight should be estimated and, before judgement is passed concerning the policy chosen, the consequences of not adjusting or another adjustment policy should be calculated (see Chapter IV).

The picture of poverty presented here tries only to take stock of its evolution, mentioning the major factors in passing. In Chapters IV and V, we will be able to go deeper by means of modelling, which is indispensable for estimating the effect specific to an adjustment policy.

An increase in poverty can take two forms. On the one hand, the number of poor people can increase although their average income does not fall; on the other hand, the gap can widen between their average income and the poverty threshold Y. In one case there is an increase in the extent of poverty, while in the other it becomes more intense. The first effect is measured by the percentage of poor in the population, the second by the poverty gap (that is, the ratio between the sum of the differences between the incomes of the poor and Y, and the sum of the incomes of all individuals). In reality, the two effects often combine but have different weights, which are of interest.

As we will show, the evolution of poverty during an adjustment period varies from country to country, and within a given country, it is necessary to distinguish between rural and urban areas since they can experience changes in opposite directions.

In the two Asian countries, there was certainly no increase in poverty, mainly as a result of factors unrelated to adjustment but also because of certain adjustment measures. There had been a clear decline in poverty in Malaysia since the early 1970s, and this trend continued during the adjustment period from 1984 to 1987. Poverty was greatest in rural areas (25 per cent were poor in 1984, compared to 8 per cent in urban areas), but the percentage of rural poor declined during adjustment (22.4 per cent in 1987), while that of urban poor remained stable. Furthermore, the intensity of poverty declined in both urban and rural areas. Thus one can conclude that conditions improved in the whole country. The good results in rural areas represented an increase in the average income of small peasants who produced paddy or coconuts, which is explained by government capital outlays in rural areas before the adjustment. The incomes of agricultural workers on large plantations also continued to increase, following multi-year wage agreements negotiated before 1984. In cities, the intensity of poverty diminished because the average income of poor households increased while the average income of all households fell. In addition, as the state did not reduce per capita social expenditure but restructured it to favour the poor, its budget policy during the adjustment added to the decrease in poverty resulting from the pre-1984 measures.

The evolution of poverty in Indonesia was similar to that in Malaysia: the improvement was just as significant and the explanatory factors are the same. The 1984 and 1987 surveys provide a detailed record showing that the percentage of poor declined from 33 to 22.1 per cent and the poverty gap from 8.5 to 4.2 per cent. Furthermore, the data on incomes, consumption and calorie intake reveal the same trends. Since the two indicators of poverty are decomposable, the contribution of decreasing inequality within each group, changes in population distribution between groups and interactions of the two phenomena were calculated. It was found that most of the decline in poverty resulted from a decrease in inequality within groups. Moreover, the great majority of the poor live in rural areas. Thus the main reason for the fall in poverty turns out to have been the decrease in inequality, following an increase in income of the poor within two groups: the peasants and agricultural workers. The decreased poverty of these two groups accounts for two-thirds of the decline in poverty at the national level. The gains by poor peasants were mainly due to government capital investments in rural areas, financed by petroleum revenue since the beginning of the 1970s, and whose effects were felt only in the 1980s. In addition, average income in the rural areas grew because of an increase in demand for labour in villages, a demand which most often came from non-agricultural enterprises. These enterprises employed the better-trained youth who, in general, had completed elementary school. This evolution of the rural labour market benefited agricultural workers, whose wages increased. To be sure, as in Malaysia, certain adjustment measures contributed to this decrease in poverty, but they played a secondary role. The devaluations and liberalisation of trade had increased agricultural prices and the ratio of these prices to those of manufactured goods. Furthermore, the government did not alter social expenditure until 1987. Nevertheless, the favourable initial conditions in 1984, resulting from the sustained growth of the 1970s and public investments, remained the primary cause of this successful struggle against poverty.

The picture of the evolution of poverty in Morocco reveals greater contrasts, with a definite improvement in rural areas but probably an aggravation of poverty in the cities. In rural areas, where 60 per cent of the poor lived in 1983, the peasants benefited from a stability of real agricultural prices, even an increase for some products, despite a jump in production. The raising of official prices contributed to this, as did the liberalisation of trade, which exercised pressure for lower prices on manufactured goods. The determining factor, however, was the leap in production of cereals and legumes as a result of the good rainfall. Since the poor peasants consume what they produce, their standard of living, which depends mainly on their harvests, improved like that of other farmers. Furthermore, poor peasants received increasingly large remittances from emigrants. This aid plays an important role. If it is assumed that half of the emigrants are from rural areas, the remittances concern 160 000 rural families out of 1 million, of which 300 000 to 350 000 are considered poor. To be sure, the adjustment policy stimulated these transfers and encouraged higher agricultural prices, but the favourable weather remains the main reason for the fall in poverty. In contrast to the experience of the two Asian countries, it was a random factor rather than a policy of public investments in the 1970s that had prevented any increase in poverty. Moreover, the percentage of poor decreased more than the intensity of poverty: it was the moderately poor peasants who benefited from the higher prices and greater transfers, while the poorest sold almost nothing and in some cases withdrew their children from school.

Poor urban households were in a less favourable situation, for several reasons. To be sure, the legal minimum wage and the wage of low-skilled workers in the modern sector were stable in real terms, and hence families untouched by unemployment maintained their purchasing power. However, numerous families were hit by the large increase in unemployment in cities, some becoming poor and others becoming poorer because of the loss of a second wage. In fact, a large family which had only one minimum wage fell below the poverty threshold. On the other hand, the evolution of average income per person working in the informal sector, estimated by the macro-micro model (there was a clear fall in 1983-84, followed by a recovery so that the 1982 level was recovered in 1986), corresponded to situations which in reality were quite different, depending on the sector. Some persons were untouched since they worked in sectors that were expanding as a result of the adjustment measures, namely, tourism, textiles, clothing and leather goods. In contrast, activities such as construction were seriously hit: for example, losses of income reached 30 per cent at Fès, according to a survey. Many families there became poor, or poorer. Since approximately 40 per cent of the urban active population works in the informal sector, it is clear that such losses of income in various activities have a strong effect on urban poverty. Moreover, although the stabilization programme did not cut government transfers to the poor, neither did it increase them in real terms to compensate for the increase in poverty.

This panorama is a little oversimplified. For example, the improvement in rural areas is an average. There was a sharp deterioration in the north, however, which resulted in riots in January 1984. In this region, poorer than the average, there is contraband activity with Ceuta and Melilla. Many persons active in the informal sector go to those cities to purchase duty-free products that they resell at traditional markets. The government tried to stop this contraband trade by imposing an exit tax of 500 dirhams. Moreover, this region suffered from a localised drought in 1983. The fall in incomes from agricultural and contraband activity suddenly increased poverty and inspired a rebellious movement. This picture should also be modified for the cities, where families hit by the crisis in construction could emigrate to make up

49

for their loss of income. Retracing these different developments would be possible only with longitudinal data on incomes of poor families. Nevertheless, it is certain that the conditions of the poor on average improved in rural areas, but deteriorated for some of them in the cities.

It is difficult to estimate the evolution of poverty in Côte d'Ivoire, for the information on incomes in 1985 does not provide the necessary historical perspective. According to these data, rural poverty is mainly localised in the savannah and eastern forest, and the urban poor are mainly found in the informal sector at Abidjan (more than three-fourths of the persons active in it are poor). In the light of the surveys on per capita non-food expenditures of households in 1979 and 1985, it appears that poverty stabilized in the rural areas. There was a much smaller increase of these expenditures in the savannah (+11 per cent) than in the eastern forest (+28 per cent). This was linked to trends in the prices of cocoa, coffee and rice, the last having increased less than the other two. By contrast, poverty clearly grew in Abidjan, where incomes in the informal sector fell sharply, for two reasons: the swelling of its numbers entailed by lay-offs in the modern sector and the fall in expenditures by employees in that modern sector. This trend was enhanced by price increases resulting from the stabilization programme on goods which weighed relatively more in the budgets of low-income households.

For different reasons, there was probably the same contrast between rural and urban regions in Ghana. First, it is necessary to recall the catastrophic growth of poverty from the beginning of the 1970s to 1983, the consequences of a self-centred socialist development policy which ruined the economy. Rural poverty certainly declined when cocoa production was restarted, beginning in 1983 under the recovery programme. During the same period, the output of food crops also increased, so that the decrease in poverty affected the whole rural population. Beginning in 1987, however, the incomes of food growers took a less favourable turn, with stagnation of production and a fall in prices relative to fertilizers and manufactured goods. It is difficult to draw up an assessment for the cities. To be sure, the many lay-offs in the modern sector impoverished these employees' families, but to a limited extent because wages had been so low before 1983 that they represented less than half of the resources of most families. Furthermore, the devaluations and price liberalisations reduced the profits of semi-clandestine small trading, which provided a living for many women. On the other hand, the Programme of Actions to Mitigate the Social Costs of Adjustment (PAMSCAD), undertaken in 1988, should raise the standard of living of the poorest persons: for example, the peasants of the north and laid-off employees. It includes projects of food aid, infrastructure (such as water supply and construction of schools and roads to villages) and aid for laid-off workers (retraining and credits to enable persons to establish themselves as artisans or planters). We do not have enough data to determine the extent to which this programme and the recovery of economic activity have offset the negative effects of certain adjustment measures on the poor.

Although we have no statistics on poverty in Ecuador, our information on incomes and public social expenditure leaves no doubt. In light of the fall in average income of small peasants and agricultural workers as well as of persons active in the urban informal sector, it is certain that poverty increased during the adjustment period in rural areas as well as in cities, where the unemployment rate doubled from 1982 to 1986. The increase in rural poverty was confirmed by the need to institute public works programmes to struggle against misery in the coastal areas which had been President Cordero's electoral base. The increase in poverty was the result of both the recession caused by the adjustment programme and the agrarian structure: the agricultural export sector benefiting from the devaluations was entirely controlled by big farmers.

Chile is a case apart, being the only country in the sample where the urban population exceeds the rural population and where the majority of the poor live in cities. Thus what matters was the evolution of urban poverty. First, it should be noted that this poverty suddenly increased beginning in 1982, with the onset of the financial crisis. This trend continued in 1983-85 during the first years of adjustment, and it did not turn around until the recovery and the increase in price of copper. The deterioration in 1983-85 was mainly the result of unemployment. More than 50 per cent of the unemployed were in the poorest 20 per cent, and more half of them received no benefits. This led the poor to look for a means of survival such as searching for work in the informal sector or, in the case of women who had children, for part-time work. Furthermore, low-skilled workers were hit by wage reductions in an economy where wages were flexible downwards, while other incomes remained relatively protected.

This impoverishment of families classified in the lowest deciles explains why it was said that there were "two Chiles", one rich and one poor, while before 1982 Chilean society had been characterised by a large middle class. It was the lower part of this class — for example, households in the 4th and 5th deciles — that was pauperised. Moreover, the reduction in social expenditure increased this phenomenon. To be sure, the programme of aid targeted at the poorest probably stabilized the conditions of families in the 1st decile, but this "safety net" did not protect the families of the 2nd, 3rd and 4th deciles, so their situation deteriorated from 1982 to 1985. This situation can in part be attributed to the adjustment policy (employment and wage flexibility without sufficient protection), but it can also be linked to the country's economic structure. It was more difficult to prevent an increase in poverty in Chile than in countries where the majority of poor are small peasants who live on what they produce and, for what they sell, benefited from an improvement in terms of trade between the agricultural and non-agricultural sectors after the implementation of certain adjustment measures.

This overview of poverty reveals that although adjustment and policy decisions sometimes play a determining role, as in Chile, factors having nothing to do with the adjustment — such as previous investments, the agrarian structure, meteorological disasters or private remittances from abroad — often play a major role, sometimes more important than the stabilization programme itself.

Note

1. The percentage for households ranked in the first three deciles is double that for households in the 7th to 10th deciles.

Chapter IV

The Lessons of Economic Modelling

The preceding chapters described in detail the crisis, the adjustment process and its apparent consequences on poverty and income distribution in the countries of the sample. Despite its precision and detail, can that description be used to deduce clear conclusions concerning the effects of the actual economic policies, or further, of policies used in one country but not in another, or even of completely new policies? Historical analysis clearly does not suffice for such an assessment.

Only experimentation could furnish this information, but that is clearly impossible. It is out of the question to apply different therapies to a country facing a crisis so as to compare their effects. Furthermore, since any economic measure or policy modifies the initial conditions, the comparison itself is unwarranted. It is also impossible to put several countries into identical crises and apply different measures in order to identify their different consequences. The initial conditions, the parameters of the crisis and the policies adopted all have historical and geographic dimensions that cannot be modified at will.

Obviously, the statistical techniques of economics (econometrics) should permit some lessons to be drawn about the effects of adjustment policies from all the identical or comparable aspects of initial conditions, national crises, adjustment policies and the observed consequences. It would still be necessary, however, to have a large enough sample of "transversal" observations (that is, in terms of countries) and also of "longitudinal" observations (that is, number of observations by country). One would also need to assume that the behaviour of the economies observed is nearly the same. Furthermore, since the economic crises that led to adjustment and the adjustment policies themselves often correspond to radical changes of behaviour, one must exercise caution in using observations outside of crisis periods or for countries which did not experience a crisis or adjustment.

The efforts to make such analyses, especially in the two World Bank evaluation reports on structural adjustment loans[1] are convincing neither in their theoretical basis (the comparableness of countries included in the sample analysed) nor in the results (a very small number of relationships analysed turn out to be really significant).

An alternative methodology would be to make experiments not with the economies themselves but with "scale models", or theoretical models of these economies. The construction of such models is itself a major enterprise since they require a degree of detail sufficient to evaluate adjustment policies. The construction of a model which will furnish information on the impact of a devaluation on a country's balance of trade will probably require only a detailed statistical analysis of time series on volume and prices of past exports and imports. On the other hand, it is a much larger enterprise to construct a model which permits studying the impact of a whole set of adjustment measures not only on large economic aggregates but also on the welfare of a population's various socio-economic groups, or, as in the study of Ecuador, the socio-economic groups important for policy decisions.

It is necessary to emphasize from the start that the construction of a theoretical scale model of a given economy is not only a major undertaking from the standpoint of the detail of the data to be used and the relationships linking these data, but it is also "risky" since modelling an economy requires making hypotheses about the functioning of the economy, that is, having a deep understanding of how it functions. One cannot imagine a model maker building a scale model of an airplane without understanding how jet engines or rudders work. Since there is always uncertainty as to the functioning of a real economy, all models run the risk of incorrectly representing basic behaviour of the real economy. Analysing an experiment on a model of a real economy requires consideration not only of the phenomena observed but also of how they may have been affected by the hypotheses used in the model's construction.

Favouring this type of approach is one of the original features of the project undertaken by the Development Centre of the OECD. Of the seven countries of the sample, five have been fully analysed by modelling, and the conclusions about the efficacy, inefficacy or redistributive effects of a particular adjustment policy are most often based on these models. The main objective of this chapter is to summarise the structure of the models, judge their adaptation to the economies analysed and examine their diagnosis of adjustment policies and of the resulting redistributive effects. Even more ambitiously, the model should also be capable of correcting the observed economic magnitudes of components which are not attributable to adjustment policies and thus, unlike the historical analysis, isolating the sole effects of adjustment policies.

This chapter is organised as follows: the first part provides a non-technical presentation of the general organisation, structure and properties of the models; the second part analyses the macroeconomic and distributive effects of the main policy instruments of stabilization and adjustment (devaluation, monetary contraction, cutting public expenditure, etc.), as these are seen by the models; and the final part is devoted to a sort of historical reconstruction. This attempts to reconstitute purely the overall effect of the adjustment policy for the modeled countries, that is to say, what would have happened if results had not been contaminated by other exogenous variables. There is also an attempt to make a general evaluation of adjustment programmes, as they were seen by the models.

1. The Structure of the Simulation Models

Although different from several points of view, the models used for Côte d'Ivoire, Ecuador, Indonesia, Malaysia and Morocco are constructed on a common principle. This principle is the linking of more or less detailed microeconomic modelling of the sectoral structure of production, prices and incomes with a macroeconomic model capable of representing and analysing the effects of the main components of the stabilization and structural adjustment policies. We begin our description of the models by their microeconomic component.

The microeconomic basis of the simulation models: computable general equilibrium

In order to represent all the complexity of the economies analysed, the various models used in this project are all basically computable general equilibrium (CGE) models[2]. The principle of these models is the Walrassian idea of making compatible, through the price system, the complex set of decisions by the economic agents who form the economy.

The structure of an elementary CGE model is described in Figure IV-1 The production side of the economy is decomposed into a certain number of sectors, each sector producing a good or service (Q_i). This production is obtained from intermediate goods (X_{ij}) and factors of production (F_{i1}) according to a "production function":

$$Q_i = G_i(X_{i1}, ..., X_{in}; \ F_{i1}, ..., F_{im})$$

The Walrassian hypothesis of perfect competition assumes that, given a system of prices of goods p_1, p_2, ..., p_n and of factors w_1, w_2, ..., w_m, each sector i maximises its profit, or its sales, p_iQ_i, less the cost of its inputs and factors of production. If the function G_i is known, one can determine from it the supply of good i, Q_is, the demand X_{ij}n for intermediate products and demand for factors F_{i1}d. All the magnitudes are functions of the system of prices of goods p_1, p_2, ..., p_n and of factors w_1, w_2, ..., w_m. There is also a function of these two sets of prices, the profit π_i, made in each of the sectors i.

After the description of the decisions taken in the production sector, the distribution of household incomes is considered next. This is crucial in the light of the objective of the model: to define redistributive effects of the adjustment policy. It is based on the "matrix of ownership" of factors F_{jk}^*, which indicates the quantity of factor j, including the labour of different types, belonging to the group of households k. If Θ_{ik} is the share of ownership of the group of households k in the profit of enterprises of sector i, the income of groups k is obtained by simple summation:

$$y_k = \sum_i \Theta_{ik}\, \Pi_i + \sum_j w_j\, F_{jk}{}^{\bullet}$$

Since the demand for factors by enterprises and their profits depend on the price system and factor payments, it is also true that the distribution of incomes among the different socio-economic groups k is a function of these same price and payment vectors.

To close the model, it remains to determine the final demand C_{ik} and the supply of factors F_{jk}^* coming from the different socio-economic groups. A simple way to proceed is to postulate a consumption function, in which the demand of household k for good i depends on the income of the group, y_k, and the prices of different goods p_1, p_2, ... p_n:

$$C_{ik} = C(y_k;\ p_1, p_2, ... p_n),$$

while the supply of factors F_{jk}^* is assumed to be exogenous. Since the incomes y_k themselves depend on the set of prices p_i and w_j, the final consumption demands of households actually appear as functions of these two sets of prices and implicitly of the quantities of factors possessed or supplied by each socio-economic group.

Assuming that the economy has no external relationships, and ignoring the roles of government and investment, equilibrium of supply and demand on all the markets should be the solution of the following set of equations:

$$\sum_k C_{jk}\,(p,w) + \sum_i X_{ij}{}^d\,(p,w) = Q_j{}^s(p,w)$$

and:

$$\sum_i F_{ij}{}^d\,(p,w) = \sum_k F_{jk}{}^{\bullet}$$

where p and w represent the set of prices of goods and of factor payments respectively. In this system of equations, the terms on the left represent demand (for final consumption and intermediate consumption in the first equation and for factors in the second), while the terms on the right describe the supply of goods and services. Under certain conditions of regularity of functions $G_i(\ )$ and $C_i(\ )$, it can be shown that there exists a unique solution of this set of two equations, that is (p^*,w^*), the corresponding "general equilibrium" of the economy. This solution is obviously a function of the set of parameters entering into the functions $G_i(\ )$ and $C_i(\ )$, that is to say, a function of the conditions of production and consumer preferences, and also of the distribution of factors in the population (F_{jk}^*) and of the property of enterprises $(_{ik})$.

Empirically, if one has the national accounts in which the flows of products and incomes are distinguished by sector, factors of production and household socio-economic groups (a social accounting matrix, or SAM), it is possible to obtain a precise estimate of functions $G_i(\ )$ and $C_i(\ )$ on the hypothesis that the economy was initially at equilibrium. Once this "calibration" has been made, the equilibrium equations can be solved for different values of the parameters or available factors. One can then empirically study how the distribution of incomes (y_k) changes as a function of the structure of factor ownership, of shocks on the technical coefficients or of the structure of household preferences. For example, how does inequality of real incomes or poverty change in relation to productivity gains in manufacturing, meteorological risks in agriculture or a change in the budget coefficients of households?

Generalising the model: the problem of macroeconomic closure

This simple analytic framework can be generalised in several ways. In the first place, it is necessary to introduce government activity, that is to say, the production of non-tradable goods and services by public employees and some intermediate consumption — and possibly its distribution by type of user — as well as the levying of various taxes and the payment of certain transfers to households. This raises a first difficulty, that of whether one should assume that the government budget is balanced. If not, should the budget deficit be financed by money creation or by borrowing from domestic economic agents? Here is a first point of encounter between the rigorously microeconomic approach followed up to now and problems that are really macroeconomic. For the moment, it will be assumed that the government budget is balanced, that it is financed by indirect exogenous taxes, at the rate t_i, on traded goods and that the corresponding income is expended in goods G_i and in wages paid to factors F_{jg} following a given structure. The rule of budget equilibrium implies that the absolute value of public expenditure satisfies:

$$\Sigma_{ti} . Q_i\ (p\ ,\ w) = \Sigma\ G_i + \Sigma\ w_j\ . F_{jg}$$

In this way, government demand for goods, services and factors becomes exogenous: it depends on the rate of indirect taxation as well as on equilibrium prices and payments. Moreover, it may be observed that the prices in the demand and supply functions now should differ in proportion to the rate of taxation. We will not go into details of this analysis, however, the present discussion being intended only to illustrate a new use of the initial model. With the introduction of the state, it becomes possible to analyse in some detail the role of budgetary policy and public expenditure in the productive apparatus and incomes of socio-economic groups. This was actually one of the ways in which models constructed under this project were used.

A second necessary generalisation concerns relations with the exterior. A simple way of representing the possible competition between imported products and domestic products on the one hand, and between exports and domestic sales on the other, is to define goods actually consumed and produced as "composite" goods, composed partly of foreign goods (or goods sold abroad) and partly of domestic goods (or goods sold within the country), and to postulate a certain elasticity of substitution between the two components. If p_i is the price of the good produced domestically and p^{oi} the price of the competing imported good, one can define a composite good consumed by domestic economic agents whose price is given by $P_i = d_i p_i + (1 - d_i)p^o_i$, and where the ratio $R_i = d_i/(1 - d_i)$ indicates the shares of domestic and imported goods in the satisfaction of domestic needs of the composite product i. The substitutability, or the competition, between the two sources is obtained by assuming a constant elasticity ε_i between the ratio R_i and the relative price p_i/p^o_i:

$$dR_i\ /R_i = \varepsilon_i\ d\ (p_i\ /p^o i\ )/(p_i\ /\ p^o i\ )$$

an elasticity of zero corresponding to the case where the domestic and imported goods are strictly complementary. In a similar way, one can obtain the substitutability, or the competition, between sales by domestic enterprises on the domestic market and exporting at a given foreign price p'_i. In this way, an increase in the domestic price p_i in relation to foreign prices brings not only an increase in imports and a decline in domestic production, but also a decline in exports and possibly a turning of domestic producers towards the domestic market.

This convenient form of representing the choices of domestic and foreign economic agents between domestic goods and foreign trade is still hiding a macroeconomic datum that is fundamental for the economies studied in this project: the exchange rate system. Clearly, the foreign prices of imported products p^o_i and exported products p'_i are based on prices observed on foreign markets in a foreign currency — for example, the American dollar — and the exchange rate e between the domestic currency and the dollar. Is this exchange rate exogenous or endogenous? If the latter, how is it fixed? If it is indexed to domestic prices (crawling peg), then how are those fixed? If it is set to balance the current account, what must be assumed about international capital movements?

A third generalisation of the initial model is necessary to incorporate the dimension of time. The model discussed above is atemporal or static; it is concerned with economic equilibrium during a unique, more or less well-defined period. If this period is a year and if the empirical calibration of the model seeks to reproduce the national and social accounts of that year, how will the model treat investments, which determine the dynamics of a real economy? Moreover, inasmuch as the objective of this research project is to analyse the structural adjustment of economies in crisis, it is hardly possible to ignore the fundamental role of investment or other essentially dynamic phenomena, like labour migrations and technological progress, in the reallocation of resources. It would be no more satisfactory for the aim of this research project to treat total investment and its sectoral distribution as exogenous or, as some do, to work within the framework of an economy enjoying stable growth, in which volume and structure of investment are endogenous and ensure a constant and equal rate of growth for all sectors.

It was thus absolutely necessary to model private investment and the dynamics it gives to an economy in a way that is compatible with the savings behaviour of economic agents. This too requires direct and explicit reference to the mechanisms of macroeconomic equilibrium: the functioning of financial markets and of bank credit, the linkages between national and international capital markets, etc.

In the light of these examples, it can be seen that the main function of the initial CGE model, which was to endogenise the price system, factor payments and, consequently, the whole distribution of income, is only partially fulfilled if the model's macroeconomic framework has not been specified.

This problem of "macroeconomic closure" of CGE models is almost as old as the models themselves. The model thus far described can determine only relative prices since only these prices count in microeconomic decisions (as long as no utility is given to money, as such). There are different ways of passing to absolutes: by choosing an arbitrary numéraire (for example, the GDP deflator), by linking domestic prices to international prices by a fixed exchange rate, or by introducing money and a demand for money simply for the purpose of a transaction (the "Cambridge" equation). Taylor and Lisy[3] showed in 1978 that the closure used has an important influence on the distribution of income and the way in which it reacts to the model's exogenous variables. The closures just mentioned could be considered simplistic compared to the macroeconomic generalisations discussed above. The logic of this research project thus led us to pursue more rigorously the links between, on the one hand, the microeconomic approach of calculable general equilibrium and its endogenisation of income distribution and, on the other, the macroeconomic phenomena at the heart of stabilization and adjustment.

The structure of the models used in the project

Since details of the models are given in the monographs on each country and in the initial paper of Bourguignon, Branson and de Melo[4], here we will indicate only the major choices of modelling.

Stabilization and structural adjustment programmes affect income distribution in three different ways. The first corresponds to modifications of the government budget and the impact on economic incentives of reforms import, customs and the exchange reforms. These effects are correctly taken into account in the medium and long term by the simple CGE models described above, which are the first constituent part of the models used in the case studies.

Second, a stabilization programme can affect income distribution through short-term effects such as a change in aggregate effective demand or in prices of financial assets like government bonds. Since the prices of those assets can directly influence investment spending, these short-term effects are naturally prolonged to the medium term. Thus nearly all the stabilization programmes analysed in this project involved cuts in public expenditure and a contraction of the money supply. These stabilization policies also lead to a decline in employment and utilised capacity, since most economies show a certain rigidity in nominal prices and wages. Of course, it is possible to introduce such rigidity in the CGE models described above, but since the financial sector generally does not figure in these models, it is impossible to take into account the effects of adjustment policies on investment and other variables via mechanisms affecting interest rates.

Third, changes in the price of financial assets lead to capital gains and losses which affect the distribution of wealth and, consequently, that of income and consumption. For example, exchange controls can be ineffective and expectations of devaluation could lead to large flights of capital. The modelling of portfolios also permits taking into account that stabilization programmes in countries with a relatively high rate of capital mobility have often led to revisions of these portfolios in favour of foreign assets and to large gains by the holders of foreign assets after devaluation.

Though short-term dynamics and the rise of expectations will not be emphasized, the models constructed for this project quantify all the relationships between these three effects of stabilization and adjustment policies on the distribution of income and wealth. It was already known that the first type of effect could be analysed with traditional CGE models, which emphasize relative prices and reallocation of resources and their impact on income distribution, and the macroeconomic extension of these models described earlier enables them to analyse the two other types of effects. More precisely, we used the standard macroeconomic framework of the IS-LM model of an open economy where the prices of assets are determined endogenously (cf. Tobin, 1969, or Branson, 1989). The model described here, which has been used in four of the seven case studies, derives from this dual tradition. We will describe the original features of this model (which we prefer to call a "maquette" because of its great structural flexibility), emphasizing its micro-macro linkage.

Taking financial assets into account

In the countries of the sample in which financial markets were the most developed, four types of assets were considered: money, domestic public debt (treasury bonds), physical assets and foreign assets. The accumulation of these assets corresponds to traditional accounting balances.

The balance of payments is written:

$$X - M - TR = e\,(\,\Delta F^{*h} - \Delta L^{*w} + \Delta R^{*} - \Delta B^{*w}\,)$$

That is, the balance of the current account (exports X, less imports, M, less current transfers, including interest on debt, TR) is equal to that of capital flows to the rest of the world (indicated by superscript asterisk ∗): the accumulation of foreign assets by domestic households ΔF^{*}_{h} , the accumulation of foreign loans by domestic enterprises, ΔL^{*}_{w} ; net government borrowing abroad, ΔB^{*}_{w}, and the net accumulation of foreign reserves by the Central Bank, ΔR^{*}. The exchange rate, e, is used to convert all these flows into domestic currency. When there is a flexible exchange rate, then ΔR^{*} is set at zero. If the exchange rate is fixed or indexed to domestic prices (a crawling peg), as was true for most of the countries studied[5] ΔR^{*} or net government borrowing ΔB^{*}_{w} should vary so as to soak up excess demand for foreign currency. If there are exchange controls, then and ΔL^{*}_{w} are exogenous and possibly zero. In Morocco's case, it was also envisaged that the balance of payments could be balanced by rationing imports; all terms on the right of the preceding identity are then endogenous (except the exchange rate, e), and equilibrium is assured by a variation of M.

The government's budget deficit is financed by borrowing from the Central Bank (money creation), B_b, from domestic households (treasury bonds), ΔB_h, or from abroad, ΔB^{*}_{w}. If G is total public expenditure and T the fiscal receipts:

$$G - T = \Delta B_b + \Delta B_h + e\Delta B^{*}_{w}.$$

Finally, an excess of savings S over investment I in the whole private sector gives rise to accumulations of cash balances, treasury bonds and foreign assets (or liabilities), and to a decrease in the outstanding domestic and foreign debts of domestic firms:

$$S - I = \Delta H_h + \Delta H_f + \Delta B_h + e(\Delta F^{*h} - \Delta L^{*}_{w}) - \Delta L_b$$

in which H_h and H_f are respectively the changes in cash balances of households and of firms (cash assets) and L_b the outstanding credit of enterprises in the domestic banking system.

By substituting the preceding expressions in the well-known identity of national accounting:

$$(S - I) + (T - G) = (X - M - TR)^{6}$$

we obtain the consolidated account of monetary operations, which leads after simplification to the identity defining money creation:

$$\Delta H = \Delta H_b + \Delta H_f = \Delta B_b + e\Delta R + \Delta L_b$$

In other words, money creation is equal to the variation of the Central Bank's credit to the government, plus the whole banking system's credit to enterprises, plus the monetisation of the variation of foreign reserves.

This accounting structure is able to represent a large variety of financial operations currently used by developing economies. Most of the time, however, some of these operations are prohibited or do not occur. For example, exchange controls can prevent private capital movements. In that case $\Delta F^{*}_{h} = L^{*}_{w} = 0$. The government's foreign borrowing is suppressed (and thus a flexible exchange rate or rationing of imports is instituted) by setting $B^{*}_{w} = 0$. The treasury bond market is $B_h = 0$. This is done in the Malaysian model in which money is the sole financial asset. On the other hand, in the Indonesian model there are several interest-bearing financial assets. A fixed exchange rate and free private capital movements suffice to represent the financial markets for countries like Côte d'Ivoire, Indonesia and Malaysia but it seemed reasonable to have a fixed exchange rate with an exogenous constraint on foreign debt for Chile after 1982 and for Ecuador after the fall in petroleum prices. Moreover, in all cases of devaluation from a "fixed" exchange rate (Morocco, Indonesia, Malaysia), it is clear that variations in reserves or the level of government indebtedness become endogenous variables.

Choosing the portfolio and real/financial arbitrage

In order to simplify the representation of financial choices, the models that include more than one asset are based on a sequence of dual alternatives (see Figure IV-2). In view of the assets in the model, the wealth constraint W is written:

$$W = Hh + PaEh + Bh/i + eF^{*}h/i^{*}$$

in which P_a is the price of the ownership of physical shares[7] E_h by households in the capital of enterprises (including individual enterprises), B_h the nominal yield of bonds held, i the domestic interest rate, F^*_h the nominal yield of foreign securities and i^* the foreign interest rate. First, the share of household wealth invested in money is determined by a conventional demand function in which the cash balances depend positively on the income of households or enterprises (transactions), the nominal domestic rate of interest[8], and in some cases by the (expected) rate of inflation. The rest of the wealth is then divided between physical capital (shares of ownership of the productive capital of firms) and financial placements (domestic or foreign bonds), on the basis of expected nominal rates of return for the two types of investment. Finally, the remaining wealth is divided between domestic and foreign securities on the same basis. The demand for each asset thus depends on the total wealth inherited — and possibly reevaluated because of observed variations in exchange or interest rates — and on the expected nominal rates of return of the various different assets, which in the main depend on the rates of inflation, devaluation, and domestic and foreign interest. It should be noted that these demands concern stocks and not flows. For this reason, for example, an expected high rate of inflation could lead households to liquidate the greater part of their financial assets and seek refuge in physical capital which, by definition, is protected from inflation, or even in foreign securities because of a crisis of confidence, as in de Janvry and Sadoulet (1991). Likewise, the expectation of a devaluation could tilt portfolios in favour of foreign securities.

The investment functions

Faced with the supply of savings by households, all the models used give a large place to an autonomous demand for investment by enterprises. These functions differ from one model to another and reflect certain national characteristics. Thus the investment functions of the Indonesian model are estimated econometrically on the basis of a specification similar to the logic of the accelerator with a correction term that depends on interest rates. Inflation has a direct influence on investment in the Ecuadorian model. The specification used in the Ivoirien and Moroccan models follows the theory of the "q ratio" of Tobin (ratio between the value — discounted according to the observed interest rate — of the sector's expected profits and the replacement value of assets). As enterprises do not always function at full capacity, the investment function also has the characteristics of the accelerator in a Keynesian system.

In all these models, public investment has an explicitly productive role in the private sector. It partly determines the coefficient of technical progress in the Indonesian and Ecuadorian models, and it adds directly to the effect of private investment in the others. In this way, the models take into account an important aspect of the arbitrage between short-term stabilization and long-term growth[9]. In sacrificing public capital outlays to adjust the balance of trade, a society is also diminishing its long-term potential for growth.

2. The Effects of the Main Macroeconomic Instruments of Stabilization

Aided by the preceding models and owing to their micro-macro linkage, the modeled case studies are all devoted to analysing the distributive impact of macroeconomic stabilization policies. Here it is important to distinguish between macroeconomic stabilization and structural adjustment, since it is principally the former which demands taking into account macroeconomic phenomena and their linkage with an economy's sectoral and social structure. Structural adjustment itself can more easily be modeled on the lines of traditional applied general equilibrium models, since it is concerned with structural variables especially likely to modify incentives and relative prices. Moreover, it should be noted that structural adjustment policies have a longer-term effect than stabilization policies. In view of the available data the case studies focused primarily on the short and medium term. Thus the macroeconomic stabilization instruments have pride of place in the analyses, and we give them the same emphasis in the synthesis which follows.

Adhering to the textbooks on open macroeconomics, the case studies considered separately or together: a) policies cutting public expenditure, b) policies cutting the money supply, and c) devaluation of the exchange rate. At this level of generality, however, it is difficult to compare the studies: the specifications for simulations of monetary contraction or budget cuts are not the same from one case study to another, because the models are different or have been used in different contexts. One study analyses a well-defined set of measures, while another is concerned with how to attain a given objective in the balance of trade or the balance of payments by using different combinations of macroeconomic instruments. We can therefore make only qualitative conclusions about the common results of the models. These are the results which appear in Tables IV-1 to IV-5 for each of the four countries of the sample analysed by a model of the type that has just been discussed.

Budget-cutting policies

Nearly all the adjustments analysed in the project have involved cuts in public expenditure — capital outlays, current expenditure or both. What can be said *a priori* about the macroeconomic and distributive effects of such measures?

On the macroeconomic level everything obviously depends on the closure specified. In a fairly Keynesian regime, cutting public expenditure should produce a decline in economic activity, an increase in unemployment and an improvement in the balance of trade, as a result of the negative income effect on imports. In a more classic regime, in which all markets adjust to equilibrium as a result of price flexibility, the exogenous decline in government demand should lead to a compensatory increase in the other components of demand through a modification of the system of prices. The main expected effect is a "crowding in" of private investment. On the whole, the cut in public expenditure leads to a growth of domestic savings; this contributes to a decrease of interest rates which in turn favours private investment[10]. The impact on the trade balance may be less favourable than in the first case, as the imported component of private investment is generally large.

On the level of income distribution, the Keynesian scenario leads to a deterioration as a result of rising unemployment and declining effective demand in the sectors where the majority of the poor are found. On the other hand, the classic scenario leads to more ambiguous results. If output does not change and if, because of a relatively inelastic labour supply, employment remains nearly stable, all the distributive effects result from a modification of prices and factor payments. The factors affected are obviously those used intensively by sectors that respond to government demand.

It is thus advisable to indicate the category of public expenditure that has been cut. The distinction between current and capital expenditures is especially important if, as several models assume, the latter are a driving force in the growth of productivity.

Four case studies explicitly analysed the effects of such cuts in public expenditure or an increase in taxes. In the case of Indonesia, a sharp 20 per cent cut in all categories of public expenditure — both current expenditure and capital outlays — led to a short- and long-term deflation. In the short term, the effect was relatively moderate because of an assumed flexibility of the price system and the rigidity of the nominal rate of exchange. These various assumed factors led to a small disinflation of prices and thus a real devaluation, which permitted a restructuring of demand to compensate for the cut in public expenditure. Although real wages are supposedly rigid, in fact the situation approximated the aforementioned classical schema in which a drop in one component of demand is compensated by an increase in another. The GDP and the average income of households fell by only 2.5 per cent. In a longer term, however, there was a greater fall in production (4.2 per cent of GDP) owing to the negative influence of the decrease in public investment on growth of productivity. Perhaps the long-term decline in the GDP could have been avoided if the budget reductions had involved only current expenditure and, on the contrary, if public investment had been increased.

Table IV-3 reveals that the long-term distributive effects of a cut in public expenditure are highly dependent on the structure of these cuts. A uniform reduction tends to favour the rural sector over the urban because the suppliers of goods and services to the government concentrate in the urban sector. However, this effect can be partially eradicated by changing the relative weights of current expenditure and capital outlays. To be sure, the Indonesia model does not take into account the social welfare losses due to a decline in current expenditure.

This unfavourable effect of a reduction in current expenditure is taken into account explicitly in the Ecuadorian model, in which the closure is closer to the Keynesian model as a result of a certain rigidity of nominal wages. Decreased demand leads to less inflation, an increase in real wages and hence increased unemployment. This effect is somewhat compensated by an increase in private investment ("crowding in" effect), owing to the reduced pressure of public expenditure on savings and a decrease in the interest rate. All socio-economic groups lose in the short term during this recession. The most well-off classes lose the most because they are directly hit by cuts in public sector employment. The losses of the urban poor result especially from cuts in public expenditure and the social services linked to them. In the long run, however, the effect of a deflationary public expenditure policy is beneficial in comparison to other types of adjustment because it offers the greatest flexibility for real wages and because of the jump in private investment, which leads to significant gains in productivity.

The analytic framework used in the Moroccan and Ivoirien models is more conventionally Keynesian in the short term. It assumes that not only nominal wages but also profit margins in the modern sectors of the economy are rigid in the short term and that enterprises prefer to adjust to a contraction in demand by leaving productive capacity unutilised rather than lowering their prices[11]. Moreover, it is assumed reasonably that a decrease in the budget deficit is accompanied by a slowing of the increase in the money supply, lessening the compensatory crowding-in effect that was seen in the case of Ecuador. As a result, the deflationary effect is greater than in the preceding examples. The effect on income distribution is also more complex. On the one hand, the owners of modern sector enterprises maintain their rate of profit by the rigidity of their prices, while purchasing power will rise for employees of modern sector who are not laid off because of the rigidity of nominal wages and price decreases, which result from the deflation in the traditional sectors of economy, notably the agricultural, food product and urban informal sectors. On the other hand, the fall in urban demand produces a deterioration in the agricultural and informal sectors' terms of trade, thus decreasing the real income of peasants, agricultural workers and persons working in the informal sector. Thus there is a substantial increase in inequality and poverty, especially if it is assumed that the unemployed share the incomes of the least favoured classes rather than those of modern sector workers. It should be noted, however, that the social costs of adjustment by budget cuts would have been greater in these two countries if the decline in social services associated with cuts in public expenditure had been taken into account, as was done for Ecuador.

The preceding observations refer to a certain extent to the "macroeconomic" effect of budget cuts and ignore the structural characteristics of a cut in the budget deficit. However, it makes a difference if the budget deficit is reduced by manipulating the "income" column in the national accounts — that is to say, taxes and duties — rather than the "expenditures". Similarly, the nature of the public expenditure concerned by the cut is also important.

The first difference is illustrated in the Moroccan study by a comparison between cutting current expenditure, public investment, the average wage of public employees (by modifying the qualification structure) or the number of public employees, and increasing customs duties and indirect taxes. Using these diverse means to achieve the same cut in the deficit of the current account has quite different effects on economic activity, income distribution and poverty. A reduction in public employment, without a change in the wages of public employees, leads to a greater reduction in economic activity and a greater increase in poverty than cutting current expenditure[12] or the average wage of public employees (see Table IV-5).

The second difference has been studied in depth in the case of Indonesia. The available data for this country permitted considerable disaggregation, which made it possible to compare the effects of a uniform, proportional cut in public expenditure with those of selective cuts in different budget categories, as well as the real average for the 1984-89 period with the figures observed in 1980. It is shown in the Indonesian study that the way in which public expenditure is reduced really influences income distribution. On the one hand, it is seen that a modification in the structure of public expenditure does not have the same effect on different socio-economic groups: the use of public educational and health services by the well-to-do, middle and poor classes is not in proportion to their incomes. On the other hand, it was confirmed that high-income non-agricultural groups are affected more by the uniform cut in all categories of current expenditure than by a reduction more oriented towards public investment[13].

Monetary contraction policies

Most stabilization programmes involve reductions in the domestic supply of money or credit. According to the traditional schema, this measure should reduce the inflation of domestic prices and increase the cost of credit, that is to say the interest rate — or the implicit rate when credit is rationed, as in the model used for Morocco. For a given rate of devaluation, the smallest rise in domestic prices will lead to a real depreciation of the currency, which can contribute to an improvement in the current account balance. An increase in the interest rate leads to a decline in investment or, if capital is sufficiently mobile, an influx of foreign capital. In the first case, a reduction in investment permits balancing the current account, on the one hand, as in the Keynesian schema, by reducing the overall level of activity, and on the other, by reducing the component of demand in which the share of imports is probably largest. In the second case the current account deficit is simply covered by the entry of foreign capital. Given the risk premium that is applied to most countries undergoing adjustment, it is unlikely that the adjustment could be confined to such movements. Among the countries of the sample, Malaysia and Indonesia certainly profited from such facilities. In the other countries, it was this very constraint which weighed heavily in the decision to undertake an adjustment policy. It is evident to international investors that the risk premium for a given country becomes prohibitive once the level of debt passes a certain threshold.

It has been seen that financial mechanisms were modeled in great detail in all the models constructed for this project. In analysing the consequences of monetary policies we saw the importance of these mechanisms. In the case of Indonesia, on the whole they lead to a certain distributive neutrality of adjustment. Monetary contraction brings down the rate of inflation, thus a real devaluation of the rupiah and an improvement in the current account balance. It also leads to a decrease in investment. In the short term, the decline in investment is compensated by increased exports and a competitive gain for domestic products. In the long term, on the other hand, this decline will entail a lower rate of growth for the economy. In both the short and the long term, however, the distributive effects of monetary contraction prove very moderate. Although the corresponding results were not provided, one would expect that interest rate fluctuations will substantially change the distribution of wealth. In particular, domestic financial property should experience a capital loss.

In the case of Ecuador, monetary policy had a short-term effect on the distribution of income rather similar to that of a cut in public expenditure, although the urban middle and upper classes were less directly affected than they were by the cutting of public expenditure. Even if it is assumed that the decline in inflation brings about an increase of investment and a drop in exports of capital, monetary contraction entails an increase in the real rate of interest and has an overall negative effect on investment and the rate of growth. It can be seen in Table IV-2 that in the medium and long term the incomes of the different socio-economic groups are in the end hardly affected by this change in the rate of growth. Thus monetary contraction appears relatively neutral with respect to income distribution. If we compare it to policy of cutting public expenditure that would lead to the same discounted value of the GDP over the whole period of simulation, the notable difference is that the urban classes are favoured and rural groups experience a small decline in income. This is due to the bias of public expenditure for non-agricultural goods as well as the concentration of public employees in cities.

The experiments conducted in the Moroccan case lead to a similar conclusion: distributive neutrality was apparently greater with a monetary contraction than with a budget cut, except when the latter touched only public investment (see Table IV-5). This conclusion also holds for Côte d'Ivoire, at least when it is assumed that the monetary authorities of this country have the autonomy necessary for a specific monetary policy. In view of the probable rigidity of capital flows to Côte d'Ivoire beginning with the years of crisis, this autonomy was probably achieved only recently, although the rules of the Union Monétaire Ouest-Africaine still limit the power of member states to create money. In any case, it was constrained before the crisis by a fixed exchange rate with the French franc and complete freedom of capital movements, a situation which, in theory, renders monetary policy inefficient[14].

Devaluation of the exchange rate

As was just seen, monetary contraction contributes to structural adjustment by causing a real devaluation of the domestic currency. Thus it could be expected that a devaluation would have distributive effects similar to those of monetary contraction. That depends on the role of monetary contraction, which actually results in a lower rate of inflation, in contrast to its effects on the interest rate, investment and capital movements, and thus on the whole financial system.

In all the modeled countries, it was assumed that the balance of trade and, more generally, the whole economy reacted immediately to all variations in the real exchange rate, rather than using the customary J-curve, which explains that a devaluation of the exchange rate leads first to a deterioration of the balance of trade — due to the rising costs of imports — then to an improvement when domestic economic agents start substituting domestic goods on a large scale for imported goods, and foreign partners increase their demand for exports. Thus the positive effect of a devaluation on the current account shown in Tables IV-1 to IV-5 should not be surprising. In reality, this can take more than a year to occur[15]. On the other hand, it is recognised that imports and exports in all the countries are sufficiently elastic in relation to relative prices of domestic and foreign goods that all devaluations, in the end, really improve the balance of trade[16].

The distributive effects of devaluation, when compared with those of other stabilization instruments, are highly dependent on the structure of foreign trade and the closure chosen. In the case of Indonesia, a more rapid devaluation of the rupiah clearly favours peasant groups to the detriment of urban and non-agricultural rural socio-economic groups. This effect is surely linked to fact that the most elastic exports in relation to the price system come from agricultural production. The effect of a devaluation on the GDP is *a priori* more ambiguous. On the one hand, other things being equal[17], it contributes to a decrease in total demand by the negative effect that the rise in prices of imported goods has on real incomes of economic agents. On the other hand, it contributes to an increase in final demand through exports and import substitution. In the case of Indonesia, this caused a very small increase in the GDP (see Table IV-3).

Conversely, in the case of Morocco, the income effect is dominant and devaluation produces a reduction of 0.6 per cent in the GDP[18]. Among the policies whose aim is reducing the current account deficit by a given amount (in foreign currency), however, a devaluation causes the least drop in the GDP and is thus the most effective. As in Indonesia, the exports which are most elastic in relation to the exchange rate come from the agricultural sector and labour-intensive manufacturing. The devaluation therefore causes a small redistribution of income in favour of peasants and urban workers. Total inequality decreases slightly and the increase in poverty is significantly less than with other stabilization instruments.

Even if Côte d'Ivoire cannot presently devalue because it is in the franc zone, we should note that an effective devaluation occurred during the adjustment period: several times between 1981 and 1983, the French government devalued the franc and, in the process, the other currencies of the franc zone. Moreover, devaluation of the CFA franc as an instrument of adjustment has been seriously considered by some international organisations. Thus it was interesting to determine experimentally the impact of a devaluation in Côte d'Ivoire.

It can be seen in Table IV-5 that the result of a nominal devaluation of 20 per cent at the beginning of adjustment has effects comparable to those observed for Morocco. The average fall in GDP during the seven-year simulation period is less than that for the policies of monetary contraction. Furthermore, devaluation tends to favour the whole agricultural sector and to be unfavourable to the urban sector, where real wages fall as a result of price rises on imported goods. In sum, there is a significant decrease in poverty compared to other experiments and less inequality of incomes.

It is believed that the same phenomenon can be distinguished in the case of Ecuador, although the authors considered it more reasonable to accompany devaluation with monetary expansion in order to "accommodate" the rise in prices of imported goods. Thus the initial recession is much less severe, but it can shown on the basis of the figures in Table IV-2 that, even in the absence of an accommodating monetary policy, the devaluation would have had a more limited initial impact than budget cuts or monetary contraction. In the longer term, however, GDP growth is lower as a result of a more marked fall in public investment at the beginning of the period. In fact, what is being observed is a greater crowding out of private investment by exports, import substitution resulting from devaluation and the disincentive effect of imported inflation.

The effect on income distribution was the same as in the other countries, that is to say, a clear redistribution in favour of the rural sector. In the end, however, the less vigorous growth of the whole economy hits agriculture, and all socio-economic groups are affected in nearly the same proportion by the external shock.

Structural measures: import duties and indirect taxation

Although most of the studies concentrate on stabilization policies rather than on structural adjustment, some of them try to evaluate the impact of a modification of the fiscal system on foreign or domestic trade. In Morocco, for example, the analysis envisaged two ways of reducing the deficit in the current account: augmenting import duties and increasing indirect taxes (assuming that imported products are subject to the same domestic tax). With fixed prices, these two sets of measures produce the same reduction of GDP in the short term. However, households are much more directly affected by increased indirect taxes than by import duties, whose effects are more diffuse. The former thus cause a large increase in poverty and inequality (see Table IV-5).

In the longer term, an increase in customs duties is preferable, being a measure which has the merit of attacking the evil at its source: the deficit in the current account. An equivalent reduction of this deficit is obtained by an increase of indirect taxes but at the cost of an extremely severe economic contraction, which involves significant reductions in real wages and household consumption: in one year the GDP falls by 1.7 per cent instead of 1.1 per cent and the poverty gap increases by 11 per cent instead of 6.6 per cent (see Table IV-5)! This result speaks well for a dual approach to adjustment. On the one hand, there should be a series of macroeconomic measures to stabilize the economy — that is, to restore the equilibrium of the balance of payments and, to a lesser extent, that of the domestic budget — which is accomplished by traditional budgetary, monetary and foreign exchange measures. On the other hand, there should be structural measures designed to re-establish the economy's full efficiency in the long term; these may conflict with the short-term objective of stabilization. For example, it may seem that economic efficiency requires reduction and equalisation of customs duties and indirect taxes, but the simulations on Morocco show that such policies lead to greater disequilibria in the short term, even though they could have some beneficial aspects in the longer term.

Another example of a structural measure is a change in the prices which the Caisse de Stabilisation of Côte d'Ivoire imposes on growers of coffee and cocoa, the country's main export products. This simulation in the Côte d'Ivoire study is considered from a budgetary perspective — increase in government revenues following a drop in prices guaranteed to growers, at constant world prices — rather than its structural side, that is, the relative decrease of some export prices. In the light of the importance of export revenues in the Ivoirien economy, it is evident that the guaranteed grower price is a powerful instrument at both the macroeconomic and structural levels. The first effect dominates in the simulations reported in Table IV-1, where the decrease in producer prices has effects comparable to those of other budget cuts, but the structural effect reveals itself in a deterioration of the balance of trade, mainly due to a decline in the volume of exports.

General appraisal

The preceding conclusions suggest that devaluation would in general be a more efficacious and equitable instrument of stabilization than would a reduction in public expenditure or of the money supply. In most of the cases considered, it has in fact been seen that, for a given objective, a devaluation leads to a smaller short-term reduction in economic activity and, since it generally favours the rural sector, to an improvement in the distribution of income. The example of Ecuador shows that a devaluation can slow investment more than other policies, in the case of an imported inflation actually caused by a monetary policy of adapting to the rise in prices of imports. On the other hand, it is probable that the positive effects of a devaluation take longer to appear than the time periods used in the models analysed, which could make this instrument more contractional in the short term.

It is not at all surprising that devaluation proves the most efficacious and equitable instrument of stabilization. After all, adjustment is above all concerned with the balance of the current account, and it is reasonable that the main parameter of this constraint prove to be a privileged instrument. That said, the experiments just analysed show that both public expenditure and monetary policies can effect a desired adjustment to an external shock. Their distributive effects are clearly less favourable, however, except for what they have in common with a devaluation policy, that is to say, the modifications of relative prices they can bring.

Concerning budget policy, the experiments on different models, notably the Indonesian and Moroccan models, show that even the definition of these policies is important and that different results are obtained in the short to medium term depending on which current expenditure or capital outlay is cut, especially if the social utility of the expenditure is explicitly taken into account.

In sum, the simulations showed that there is an appreciable difference in the social costs of various instruments of macroeconomic adjustment or stabilization. Various combinations of economic policies could lead to a given macroeconomic objective — for example, restoring equilibrium to the balance of payments and reducing debt — but with quite different social costs and indirect effects. The choice of such a combination involves a large degree of freedom, and the choice of a particular adjustment policy should thus be highly specific for the country in question.

3. Simulating Reality and Other Experiments

As already mentioned, another advantage of the type of simulation model constructed for this project is their capability, on the one hand, of simulating the evolution of income distribution during the structural adjustment period, when the statistical information is not available directly, and on the other, of isolating what is due to the adjustment practices from that which is attributable to exogenous variations, for example, the international situation and the impact of weather conditions. Owing to their structure, the models dealing with Ecuador and Indonesia did not use these possibilities. On the other hand, there was a quite detailed analysis in the case of Morocco and to a lesser extent for Côte d'Ivoire.

Simulation of changes in income distribution

In the case of Côte d'Ivoire, the distribution of income seems to have been modified considerably during the period of adjustment, as a result of measures in the adjustment programme and of independent external shocks. Thus the reference simulation (Table IV-1) shows that the situation of employees in the modern sector deteriorated, that the entrepreneurs maintain their position, and that in 1982-84 there was a marked dip in real income of farmers (mainly due to drought) and persons working in the informal sector (a repercussion of the drought, which caused migration to urban areas). In the absence of continuous data on the incomes of these different classes of agents, these results are in themselves interesting since they show that an adjustment period can be marked by quite significant changes in the distribution of income, at least if the internal inequality of each of the socio-economic classes studied did not, in reality, move in a direction opposite to that of inequality between these classes.

The same results could be analysed in the case of Morocco (Table IV-4). This is less interesting, however, because for this country, unlike Côte d'Ivoire, there is some information concerning the real evolution of inequality between the main socio-economic classes during the adjustment period; the study's author ascertained that these changes corresponded to those predicted by the model. In this case, what counts most is the "counterfactual" analysis of the adjustment policy's effects on the distribution of income.

The overall distributive impact of adjustment policies

The main difficulty in assessing the overall effect of adjustment policies, independently of the variations of other exogenous variables, is to define what would have been the economic policy followed in the "absence" of adjustment. As observed in an earlier chapter, such a refusal to adjust could simply correspond to continued and increasing recourse to foreign credit. If the deterioration in the terms of trade turns out to be permanent and if the country's creditors question its solvency, however, it is clear that this practice is not viable beyond a certain period. At that point, the country must "adjust" in one fashion or another, that is to say, it must stop borrowing and have a balanced current account. That can be done in different ways, some of them corresponding precisely to the stabilization measures analysed throughout this work. There can also be much harsher but less efficient measures. When there are no foreign reserves and an excess demand for foreign currency, the harshest adjustment is simply to ration the available foreign currency by controlling imports. Thus a good definition of not adjusting would be the case of a country which retains all of its budgetary and monetary policies and its initial exchange rate (fixed nominally or by a crawling peg), but rations imports because of the lack of foreign currency. In fact, this occurred in Morocco in 1983 and during part of 1984. Under these conditions, an overall analysis of an adjustment policy becomes an exercise in "comparative dynamics" between the scenario of not adjusting, which has just been described, and the reference simulation in which all economic magnitudes are at their real level.

Table IV-6 compares a policy of not adjusting with that which really was implemented in Morocco in the 1984-86 period. The comparison is striking. If one first takes the case in which the country purely and simply ignored its problems by finding a generous creditor — or rather donor, since there is a low probability that the new loans will be repaid — one finds that the GDP per capita at the end of four years would have been 5 per cent greater than it was in reality. As this increase in income affects the whole population, there would have been much less poverty than in reality. The price paid for this absence of adjustment measures is mainly reflected in an 11 per cent increase in the public debt.

On the other hand, if a government had done nothing before being confronted with a liquidity crisis on the foreign exchange market, and then introduced rationing of imports, as Table IV-6 shows, the situation would have become much more disastrous than in reality, and there would have been a large increase of inequality and poverty, especially among the most destitute. After four years, the per capita GDP would have been 12 per cent below its reference level, the budget deficit would have more than doubled because of a decline in fiscal receipts and the number of poor would have increased more than 40 per cent! The most fortunate class would have been sheltered, since it would have appropriated the rent derived from import rationing, as is assumed in the model.

This table, which unfortunately is available only for Morocco (it is possible to make some gross estimates from the published figures for Ecuador), is very revealing. On the one hand, it is based on a rigorous concept of "no adjustment", which should not, as is often done, be confused with the *status quo ante*, or even with a continuation of the policy in place before the crisis and adjustment. The problem of

67

the crisis of 1980s was that the deterioration of the terms of trade proved more permanent than the policymakers had believed, that the rise in interest rates proved to be long-lasting and, even more important, that most of the heavily indebted countries lost their access to the international capital market for a rather long time. One way or another an adjustment was thus necessary. On the other hand, the main lessons to be drawn from Table IV-6, in comparison with the other tables of this chapter, is that adjustment (whether voluntary or under the compulsion of international agencies) was obviously less costly in terms of macroeconomic performance and poverty than a rigid policy under which a government would simply have rationed the entry of imported goods.

In search of optimal adjustment

The models utilised are instruments which should permit governments to "optimise" the adjustment policies by combining the different elementary measures — devaluation, contracting the money supply, cutting public expenditure, etc. — in a certain way, which could be modified in the course of time or implemented at different times with respect to the start of the economic crisis.

The modelling exercises carried out in this project lead to some agreement about the ranking of the measures considered. In most of the cases, a devaluation is shown to be superior to other measures, given its capability of correcting the evolution of the current account while favouring the poorest, or at least the rural sector. The studies of Ecuador, Morocco and, to a lesser extent, Indonesia indicate that monetary contraction policies have a rather neutral effect in the short term: they allow substantial rebalancing while requiring fairly uniform sacrifices from the population. To the contrary, policies cutting public expenditures often appear to change the relative levels of welfare of the population, especially when the use of government services financed by these expenditures is taken into account.

From this beginning, it seems that an optimal "cocktail" could be drawn up, under which adjustment in the short term would consist of a devaluation without any compensation via monetary policy and a reduction of public expenditures that are not targeted to the poorest groups. In the longer term, structural adjustment measures take over, ensuring that the fundamental causes of maladjustment are rooted out.

Unfortunately, this simple and apparently efficacious conclusion must be approached with great caution. That is another lesson of the modelling exercises. The macroeconomic and distributive effects of certain measures can depend in large measure on the functioning of the particular economy in question. It would have been difficult to envisage a devaluation or monetary contraction in Côte d'Ivoire; the great international mobility of capital in Indonesia cushioned adjustment in that country; and the Ecuadorian inflationary ambience was able to modify the effects of devaluation and contraction of the money supply, by comparison with what was observed in other countries. For the most part, therefore, the specific characteristics of each country are reflected in the conclusions to be drawn from the modelling exercises summarised in this chapter.

A final precaution to take into account in determining an optimal adjustment policy concerns the objective function or additional constraints which derive from the political situation. The Ecuadorian study and its utilisation of the model are very instructive in this respect. The objective of maximising a certain social utility function could be incompatible with the constraints imposed by the politics of distribution and redistribution of income. For example, the middle class or public employees could oppose, as was seen in several countries, measures targeted exclusively to the poorest groups or to the rural sector. In that case, even the notion of optimising should be abandoned for a concept that is vaguer from the standpoint of social utility, but is politically more operational. One contribution of the present project was to have shown in the rigorous framework of a micro-macro model how the political conditions can impose very strict constraints on economic policy concerning stabilization and adjustment.

Notes and References

1. See *Adjustment Lending Report*, PPR, World Bank, Washington, D.C., 1989 and 1990.
2. For a general introduction to these models, see Dervis, de Melo and Robinson (1987)
3. L. Taylor and F. Lisy, "Vanishing Income Redistribution: Keynesian Clues About Model Surprises in the Short Run", *Journal of Development Economics*, 1979.
4. See OECD Development Centre Technical Paper No. 1 and "Adjustment and Income Distribution: A Micro-Macro Model for Counterfactual Analysis", *Journal of Development Economics*, 1992.
5. Indonesia and Malaysia are exceptions to this rule.
6. This relationship is obtained from the accounting identity:

    $$Y = C + I + G + X - M$$

    in which Y is the GDP. This becomes the national income if we subtract the transfers abroad, TR, from Y. If we subtract taxes, T, from the national income, this becomes the available income which decomposes into private consumption, C, and savings, S:

    $$Y - TR - T = C + S$$

    By eliminating Y from the two identities, we obtain the indicated relationship.
7. No formal stock exchange is modeled, so that E_h represents direct ownership of physical capital by households and the price P_n is equal to the cost of replacing the whole of the physical capital.
8. Or the expected average rate of return on other assets.
9. This modelling of the productive role of public investment follows the analysis of the influence of public expenditure on growth, undertaken theoretically and empirically in recent years in the literature on endogenous growth. For example, see Barro (1990).
10. This effect may not appear in case of perfect mobility of capital, the available savings being invested abroad rather than in the domestic economy. In such a situation, overall demand is re-established through a general lowering of domestic prices and a real depreciation of the currency.
11. A number of hypotheses are considered in the original study on Morocco, but only the case of rigid nominal wages and prices is considered here.
12. It is true that cuts in social services which correspond to the current expenditure are not taken into account. On the other hand, there is probably a certain complementarity between the number of public employees and current expenditure.
13. It is true that the long-term distributive effects of a reduction in capital expenditure are not taken into account.
14. According to the Mundell-Flemming model, all money creation is transformed into outflow of capital and conversely.
15. This certainly did not occur in Morocco, where devaluation clearly produced an immediate improvement in the balance of trade.
16. This refers to the Marshall-Lerner condition in the theory of international trade. It is probably in Côte d'Ivoire that the elasticities of foreign trade in relation to the exchange rate are lowest. However, even for this country the Marshall-Lerner condition appears to be satisfied overall.
17. Monetary policy in particular.
18. The difference in relation to Indonesia also arises from the fact that the macroeconomic closure of the Morocco, as reported in Table IV-5, is much more Keynesian in the short term.

Table IV-1. Simulation of adjustment policies: Côte d'Ivoire 1980-1986 (%)

	BR[a] base	SW[b] wage	SE[c] exports	SD[d] devaluation
GDP[1]	-0.5	-0.5	-0.4	-0.4
Budget deficit/GDP[2]	-6.7	-4.8	-5.1	-3.3
Current account/GDP[2]	-14.1	-12.7	-14.3	-9.8
Commercial balance/GDP[2]	+1.5	+3.6	-1.4	+5.5
External debt/GDP[3]				
public	47.4	40.3	46.6	32.5
private	63.0	64.4	68.6	65.5
Debt service[5]	16.7	15.8	16.8	14.8
Interest rate[2]	10	9.8	9.8	13.6
Real devaluation[2]	1.3	1.6	2.3	1.8
Consumer prices[1]	7.3	7.2	6.3	9.8
GDP deflator[1]	7.1	6.7	6.0	9.4
Private consumption/GDP[2]	57.9	56.4	56.7	55.8
Exports/GDP[2]	45.7	43.6	42.3	45.2
Imports/GDP[2]	37	36.9	36.6	35.9
Investment/GDP[2]	19.8	19.9	20.3	18.5
Levels of capacity utilisation[2]	50.9	50.6	51.1	49.3
Unemployment rate[2]	5.4	5.6	5.5	4.6
Poverty gap[4](%)	14.2	15.0	17.8	14.2
Theil index[4]	54.6	49.6	70.0	48.0

1.   Average annual growth rate.
2.   Average 1980-1986.
3.   Level in 1986.
4.   Average 1981-1986.
5.   Public and private debt servicing, as a percentage of exports; average 1980-1986.

a.   Reference simulation.
b.   Drop in modern sector wages.
c.   Reduction of export prices.
d.   20 per cent devaluation of the exchange rate in 1981.

Table IV-2. Ecuador - Monetary and budgetary adjustment policies in response to a crisis in the terms of trade and indebtedness

	Base values[a]	Reference			Adjustment by devaluation			Budgetary adjustment			Monetary adjustment		
	Year 1	Year 2	Year 3	Year 7	Year 2	Year 3	Year 7	Year 2	Year 3	Year 7	Year 2	Year 3	Year 7
GDP													
Growth in volume of GDP*	3.4	3.4	3.1	2.6	-0.1	-2.1	0.4	-3.0	-0.6	1.3	-2.3	-0.5	0.9
Cumulative growth	293 341	3.4	6.6	18.9	-0.1	-2.2	-1.8	-3.0	-3.6	2.8	-2.3	-2.8	1.5
Public deficit/GDP	4.0	-3.5	-5.3	-1.3	76.6	113.0	160.9	-16.9	0.0	-5.0	107.6	130.6	140.5
Money													
Money supply*	28.0	30.0	30.0	30.0	40.0	40.0	40.0	40.0	40.0	40.0	25.0	25.0	25.0
Inflation rate*	25.0	26.2	26.5	27.2	46.7	46.1	40.3	48.3	41.7	38.8	32.4	26.3	24.5
Anticipated real interest rate**	0.0	-0.3	0.0	3.8	22.5	29.8	43.0	-0.1	3.7	7.7	34.4	40.5	46.0
Private investment	41 949	2.8	5.2	13.2	-39.3	-47.3	-48.5	-28.7	-33.2	-27.2	-39.2	-40.6	-37.5
Balance of payments													
Exchange rate*	25.0	25.0	25.1	25.3	75.3	42.4	39.8	81.1	38.5	38.0	54.3	24.0	24.0
Exports ($)	73 797	4.2	8.4	24.1	10.8	10.2	12.8	12.0	12.6	21.8	8.4	8.8	15.9
Imports ($)	74 526	3.6	7.0	20.9	-14.8	-16.8	-15.9	-16.2	-16.5	-10.1	-15.8	-15.9	-11.8
Current account deficit/GDP	4.9	-6.4	-12.3	28.7	-33.6	-39.0	-38.7	-48.1	-49.3	-53.0	-25.6	-25.6	-32.6
Capital flight	4 900	8.9	16.0	35.0	-27.5	-27.2	-45.6	5.2	0.2	-8.4	-50.5	-57.6	-63.0
Employment													
Employment	1 593	0.3	0.4	0.7	2.5	-4.7	-4.7	0.0	-5.5	-1.6	-4.0	-7.0	-2.8
Average real wage	90	4.4	8.9	26.7	-6.7	1.1	1.1	-8.9	-3.3	-1.1	0.0	4.4	3.3

	Base values[a]	Reference			Adjustment by devaluation			Budgetary adjustment			Monetary adjustment		
	Year 1	Year 2	Year 3	Year 7	Year 2	Year 3	Year 7	Year 2	Year 3	Year 7	Year 2	Year 3	Year 7
Incomes													
Small farmers	33 968	3.8	7.4	20.8	0.2	-1.6	-2.5	-1.9	-2.0	3.8	-1.6	-2.0	1.3
Medium farmers	11 325	3.7	7.0	18.7	2.4	0.8	-3.0	1.3	2.1	6.9	0.0	-0.9	0.6
Large farmers	13 094	3.4	6.5	16.9	2.8	0.8	-3.7	1.8	2.4	6.6	0.0	-1.2	-0.2
Other rural	19 251	3.6	7.0	19.9	-0.4	-3.3	-3.4	-3.1	-4.6	1.0	-2.6	-3.4	0.5
Urban, low education	70 912	3.7	7.3	21.2	-1.6	-3.7	-2.0	-4.7	-5.9	0.6	-3.2	-3.3	1.7
Urban, medium education	55 501	4.0	7.9	23.4	-2.9	-4.2	-2.1	-7.2	-7.8	-1.6	-3.8	-3.4	1.5
Urban, higher education	37 893	4.6	9.1	27.0	-3.7	-4.0	-2.0	-10.1	-10.1	-4.6	-3.7	-2.9	1.5
Well being (income + public services)													
Small farmers	35 483	3.7	7.2	20.3	0.3	-1.4	-2.0	-2.5	-2.6	3.2	-1.5	-1.8	1.6
Medium farmers	11 665	3.6	6.9	18.4	2.3	0.8	-2.7	0.8	1.6	6.4	0.0	-0.7	0.8
Large farmers	13 486	3.3	6.4	16.7	2.8	0.9	-3.3	1.3	1.9	6.1	0.0	-1.0	0.1
Other rural	21 294	3.4	6.6	18.9	-0.2	-2.7	-2.2	-4.4	-5.6	-0.1	-2.3	-2.8	1.3
Urban, low education	77 705	3.5	6.9	20.1	-1.3	-3.1	-1.1	-5.7	-6.7	-0.3	-2.8	-2.8	2.3
Urban, medium education	60 557	3.8	7.5	22.3	-2.5	-3.6	-1.2	-8.0	-8.4	-2.3	-3.4	-2.9	2.1
Urban, higher education	38 778	4.5	8.9	26.6	-3.6	-3.8	-1.8	-10.2	-10.2	-4.8	-3.6	-2.8	1.6

*   Growth rate compared with previous year.

**   Value.

These figures (apart from those lines marked with * or **) are percentage variations compared with year 1.

a.   In millions of sucres, except for growth rate.

Table IV-3a. Indonesia: simulation of various adjustment policies (short term)

	Reference	Pol. 1[a]	Pol.2-1[b]	Pol.2-2[c]	Pol.3[d]	Pol.4[e]	Pol.5-1[f]	Pol.5-2[g]
1	100.0	97.49	99.16	99.24	101.09	100.87	99.60	100.54
2	100.0	99.04	99.47	100.04	100.58	97.66	100.95	98.79
3	100.0	99.35	99.76	100.27	100.27	98.38	100.76	99.02
4	100.0	99.21	99.60	99.80	100.35	101.18	100.01	99.92
5	100.0	99.11	99.54	99.62	100.39	102.17	99.70	100.29
6	100.0	95.80	99.38	99.19	101.04	97.88	99.21	100.66
7	100.0	93.60	94.71	94.75	105.48	99.64	100.01	99.93
8	100.0	94.56	98.51	98.32	102.01	97.54	98.94	101.04
9	100.0	93.30	95.85	95.87	104.56	99.38	99.13	101.09
11	4 266.56	2 478.79	4 500.46	4 529.62	4 128.58	3 858.25	4 256.80	4 255.89
12	6 026.90	6 952.09	7 064.94	7 075.68	5 007.19	6 284.52	5 958.19	6 125.70
13	2 155.44	3 084.88	2 153.08	2 125.29	2 132.48	1 679.61	1 022.05	3 461.62
14	-6 422.00	-5 563.67	-6 654.90	-6 261.06	-5 537.87	-5 537.87	-5 278.85	-7 717.51
15	19 235.00	19 474.94	19 129.71	19 129.19	19 323.60	19 699.46	19 626.02	18 795.36
16	22 037.00	21 472.32	22 144.32	22 145.61	21 977.69	21 639.66	21 348.50	22 809.34
17	9 074.60	9 454.94	9 001.39	8 994.17	9 171.58	8 671.92	7 713.31	10 491.02
18	9 905.20	8 871.93	10 949.95	10 949.95	8 871.93	9 905.20	9 905.20	9 905.20
19	25 920.56	24 132.79	26 154.46	26 183.62	25 782.58	25 512.25	25 910.80	25 909.89
20	100.0	95.85	100.99	100.98	99.30	112.99	95.46	105.6

Per capita shares of socio-economic groups in total income

	Reference	Pol.1[a]	Pol.2-1[b]	Pol.2-2[c]	Pol.3[d]	Pol.4[e]	Pol.5-1[f]	Pol.5-2[g]
2	5.29	5.45	5.37	5.40	5.20	5.19	5.36	5.20
3	5.44	5.62	5.54	5.57	5.34	5.38	5.51	5.37
4	11.94	12.32	12.13	12.15	11.71	12.13	11.98	11.88
5	17.66	18.21	17.95	17.95	17.34	18.13	17.68	17.65
6	9.67	9.64	9.81	9.79	9.56	9.51	9.64	9.70
7	11.71	11.40	11.32	11.31	12.07	11.72	11.75	11.65
8	15.24	14.99	15.33	15.29	15.21	14.94	15.14	15.34
9	23.05	22.37	22.55	22.54	23.57	23.01	22.94	23.21
Total	100.0	100.0	100.0	100.0	100.0	100.0	100.0	100.0

74

Table IV-3b. Indonesia: simulation of various adjustment policies (long term)

	Reference	Pol.1	Pol.2-1	Pol.2-2	Pol.3	Pol.4	Pol.5-1	Pol.5-2
1	100.0	95.89	100.94	101.08	98.82	100.19	98.88	101.29
2	100.0	97.58	100.67	101.38	99.05	98.24	100.14	99.69
3	100.0	98.03	100.77	101.38	98.95	98.82	100.05	99.82
4	100.0	98.50	99.96	100.05	99.77	100.94	99.68	100.30
5	100.0	98.61	99.65	99.55	100.08	101.69	99.51	100.52
6	100.0	94.25	101.07	100.93	98.84	98.06	98.79	101.14
7	100.0	92.29	96.25	96.26	103.58	99.26	99.24	100.78
8	100.0	92.72	100.69	100.59	99.23	97.51	98.40	101.64
9	100.0	91.38	98.15	98.25	101.71	98.70	98.34	101.92
11	3 892.51	2 214.95	3 908.45	3 946.18	3 987.15	3 618.79	4 000.47	3 751.32
12	4 009.70	4 780.81	5 208.14	5 224.46	2 794.54	4 149.64	3 859.52	4 190.39
13	-1 161.82	-497.30	-916.93	-952.20	-1 463.23	-1 797.52	-2 399.69	338.22
14	-2 730.69	-1 717.66	-2 991.52	-2 993.97	-2 523.92	-1 821.27	-1 600.78	-4 089.53
15	16 071.37	16 250.10	16 179.49	16 173.92	15 907.58	16 428.09	16 330.79	15 746.95
16	15 551.92	14 781.71	15 892.32	15 889.17	15 210.65	15 033.67	14 750.31	16 498.09
17	9 788.33	9 849.38	10 068.91	10 049.37	9 467.51	9 142.62	8 204.73	11 578.47
18	8 053.10	7 019.83	9 097.85	9 097.85	7 019.83	8 053.10	8 053.10	8 053.10
19	31 385.28	25 513.82	31 441.07	31 573.10	31 716.53	30 427.26	31 763.12	30 891.11
20	100.0	97.13	98.53	98.52	102.08	114.12	96.60	104.39

Shares of socio-economic groups in total income

	Reference	Pol.1	Pol.2-1	Pol.2-2	Pol.3	Pol.4	Pol.5-1	Pol.5-2
2	5.33	5.49	5.40	5.43	5.25	5.27	5.39	5.26
3	5.47	5.66	5.55	5.58	5.39	5.45	5.53	5.41
4	11.91	12.37	11.98	11.98	11.82	12.10	11.98	11.82
5	17.57	18.28	17.62	17.59	17.50	17.99	17.65	17.48
6	9.71	9.65	9.87	9.85	9.55	9.58	9.68	9.72
7	11.71	11.40	11.34	11.34	12.07	11.71	11.73	11.69
8	15.29	14.95	15.49	15.47	15.10	15.01	15.19	15.38
9	23.02	22.20	22.74	22.76	23.31	22.89	22.86	23.24
Total	100.00	100.0	100.0	100.0	100.0	100.0	100.0	100.0

76

Incomes

1. Real income (reference = 100) GDP per capita
2. Agricultural wages
3. Small farmers
4. Medium farmers
5. Large farmers
6. Other rural, low education
7. Other rural, middle and higher education
8. Urban, low education
9. Urban, middle and higher education

Macroeconomic variables

11. Foreign public borrowing (in dollars)
12. Government savings (real)
13. Total foreign loans (in dollars)
14. Current account (balance) (in dollars)
15. Exports (in dollars)
16. Imports (in dollars)
17. Private investment (real)
18. Public investment (real)
19. Foreign public debt (in dollars)
20. Price index

a. Policy 1   Uniform reduction by 20 per cent of public expenditure.
b. Policy 2.1   Uniform reduction by 20 per cent of current public expenditure and increase by 27 per cent of public investment.
c. Policy 2.2   Uniform reduction by 20 per cent of current public expenditure and increase by 50 per cent of public investment in agriculture and by 23 per cent of other public investment.
d. Policy 3   Uniform reduction by 20 per cent of public investment and increase by 16 per cent of current public expenditure.
e. Policy 4   Devaluation of 20 per cent (nominal).
f. Policy 5.1   Reduction by 15 per cent of money supply.
g. Policy 5.2   Increase by 15 per cent of money supply.

77

Table IV-4. Morocco: Simulated evolution of income distribution (reference simulation)

		1980	1981	1982	1983	1984	1985	1986
Theil	Simulated[a]	46.3	47.0	44.0	50.4	48.2	44.6	44.0
Theil	Simulated[b]	39.4	38.9	37.5	44.1	41.1	37.1	37.5
Percentage of poor	Simulated[a]	37.9	40.9	37.6	40.2	42.9	37.9	36.2
Percentage of poor	Simulated[b]	32.3	35.0	32.4	35.4	38.1	32.6	31.1
Poverty gap*	Simulated[a]	7.3	8.8	7.4	8.1	9.3	8.2	7.3
Poverty gap*	Simulated[b]	4.8	5.5	4.7	5.4	6.2	4.7	4.2
Average income by socio-economic group								
Employers		100.0	95.0	92.0	110.0	94.0	97.0	101.0
Medium-large farmers		100.0	104.0	113.0	110.0	112.0	118.0	125.0
Smallholders		100.0	100.0	102.0	100.0	98.0	116.0	116.0
Employees[a]		100.0	96.0	94.0	89.0	89.0	94.0	90.0
Employees[b]		100.0	89.0	94.0	88.0	87.0	79.0	83.0
Agricultural workers		100.0	104.0	104.0	95.0	93.0	118.0	118.0
Urban informal sector workers		100.0	86.0	95.0	89.0	78.0	98.0	103.0

a. The unemployed are considered separately and receive no income.
b. The unemployed are grouped with employees in the modern sector.
* Share of the total income of the population necessary to bring all the poor up to the poverty threshold.

78

Table IV-5. Morocco: Means of reducing the current account deficit by 1 billion dirhams. Deviation from reference (1981)

	Current public spending	Public investment spending	Average public sector wage	Public sector employment
GDP	-16.4 %	-17.5 %	-11.4 %	-10.2 %
Household consumption	-0.9	-1.0	-0.8	-2.2
Exports	-0.7	-0.9	-2.4	-2.4
Imports	+3.3	+3.3	+3.7	+3.7
Investment	-2.7	-2.7	-2.5	-2.5
Unemployed	-3.7	-9.3	-3.2	-3.3
Current account deficit	+5.4	+6.8	+5.1	+14.4
Budget deficit	-11.8	-11.8	-11.8	-11.8
GDP deflator	-5.3	-5.4	-8.5	-8.3
Theil[a]	-1.7	-1.6	-3.6	-2.1
Theil[b]	+2.6	+1.2	-0.1	+3.0
Percentage of poor[a]	+2.0	-0.1	-2.0	-0.2
Percentage of poor[b]	+3.4	+1.9	+2.5	+4.3
Poverty gap[a]	+1.4	+1.1	+2.0	+2.5
Poverty gap[b]	+3.4	+4.1	+5.8	+9.7
	+1.7	+1.9	+4.5	+4.7

a.   The unemployed are considered separately and receive no income.
b.   The unemployed are grouped with employees in the modern sector.

Table IV-5. (continued)

	Money supply	Exchange rate	Import duties	Indirect taxes
	-3.5 %	-7.0 %	+60.0 %	+0.02 %
GDP	-1.0	-0.6	-1.1	-1.7
Household consumption	-1.1	-2.0	-1.8	-3.1
Exports	+3.3	+6.5	+1.8	+1.7
Imports	-2.7	-2.9	-3.3	-3.4
Investment	-9.3	-6.2	-5.3	-4.1
Unemployed	+7.0	+4.4	+6.3	+10.2
Current account deficit	-11.8	-11.8	-11.8	-11.8
Budget deficit	+2.8	-3.1	-6.3	-11.0
GDP deflator	-1.6	+2.5	-0.6	-1.2
Theil[a]	+1.2	-1.1	+1.3	+2.3
Theil[b]	-0.1	-2.0	0.0	+0.5
Percentage of poor[a]	+1.9	+0.7	+3.3	+5.6
Percentage of poor[b]	+1.1	+0.7	+3.0	+5.2
Poverty gap[a]	+4.1	+2.6	+6.6	+11.0
Poverty gap[b]	+1.7	+1.1	+5.6	+9.5

a.   The unemployed are considered separately and receive no income.
b.   The unemployed are grouped with employees in the modern sector.

Table IV-6. Simulation of non-adjustment. Deviation from reference (%)

	1983	1984	1985	1986
GDP	-5.7	-7.0	-4.6	-12.5
Household consumption	-1.6	-0.6	-0.0	-4.9
Exports	-27.8	-29.3	-26.6	-45.1
Imports	-21.8	-23.1	-16.7	-36.9
Investment	-18.8	-24.5	-11.2	-39.8
Unemployed	+29.8	+32.0	-6.0	-41.0
Current account deficit	-39.0	-29.5	-23.8	surplus
Budget deficit	+50.2	+40.2	+39.4	+137
GDP deflator	-1.1	-2.9	-0.1	-4.8
Public debt	-4.3	-5.2	-4.6	-5.8
Theil[a]	+38.9	+46.9	+39.0	+90.0
Theil[b]	+28.8	+36.2	+31.1	+60.5
Percentage of poor[a]	+16.5	+18.9	+16.4	+47.0
Percentage of poor[b]	+12.4	+14.1	+20.3	+40.4
Poverty gap[a]	+29.9	+30.7	+16.8	+76.3
Poverty gap[b]	+27.3	+28.5	+34.5	+90.3

a.   The unemployed are considered separately and receive no income.
b.   The unemployed are grouped with employees in the modern sector.

Figure IV-1. Structure of an Elementary CGE Model

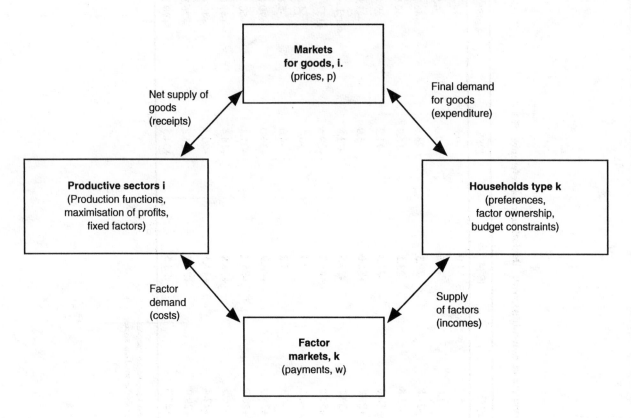

Figure IV.2. **Diagram for determining the composition of household portfolios**

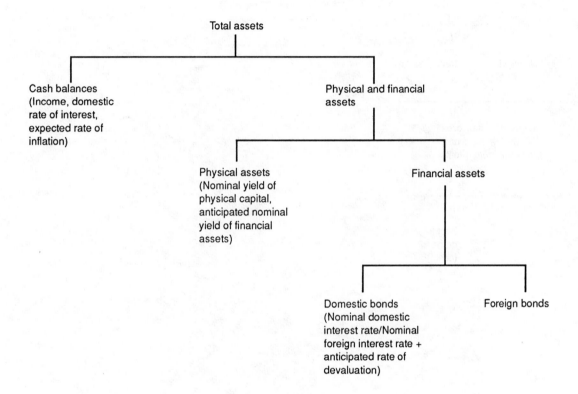

Chapter V

Summary and Recommendations

1. The Political Dimension of Adjustment

The analysis of disequilibria and crisis, the picture of the evolution of incomes during adjustment and the presentation of the modelling intentionally remained within an economic perspective. This is no longer possible, however, in this last chapter, which is devoted to policy recommendations that would be completely unrealistic if the political dimension of adjustment were not taken into account.

Several works[1] have recently been published on the political feasibility of adjustment programmes, studies which draw specifically on political science. Taking into account their contributions, we must examine the interactions of the three aspects of adjustment: the economic, social and political. In one sense, all the earlier chapters had a common objective of underscoring the relationships between the economic and social, the latter comprising incomes, unemployment, social services and poverty. As soon as we tackle practical findings, however, it is necessary to integrate the political aspects. Before taking up the means and alternatives available to governments, we will briefly recall the political contours.

The political context proves important for understanding the history of adjustment, whether it involves a choice of unbalanced growth, increasingly costly in terms of indebtedness, or the negotiation of adjustment programmes.

The classic crisis arises from the combination of an external shock and a fragile initial situation (see Chapter I.1) linked to large foreign indebtedness from the 1970s. This error was analysed economically: governments developed false expectations as a result of the boom in raw material prices and, after the fall in prices, financed an increasing proportion of large investments by foreign loans, assuming that this drop had been only a temporary accident.

It is also possible, however, to interpret this behaviour politically. There could have been two other possible reactions. The first would have been to acquire sufficient public savings to finance these investments. That would have made it necessary to increase taxation of high incomes and reduce current expenditure. But the groups concerned by such a fiscal reform often have close ties with the government, whether it is an authoritarian or democratic system, as was the case with the coalition in Ecuador supporting President Cordero, which of course opposed this reform. On the other hand, a reduction in current expenditures affects public employees directly (wages) or indirectly (working conditions), and consequently touches the urban middle class which has considerable influence in the administration and political life. In these circumstances, economic growth on credit could be an intentional error since it permits the government to reconcile growth with the interest of these influential groups.

The second possibility, letting the private sector take over investment, also would create problems. First, this substitution would very probably have been partial, and total investment would have been much smaller. On the other hand, this privatisation of investment would have demanded an increase in interest rates to stimulate savings in countries where deposits are under-remunerated, as in Côte d'Ivoire and Morocco, but such a rise would have restrained investment. In compensation, a financial liberalisation would have augmented bank deposits and hence the resources for investment. Above all, such a step would have reduced the influence of high government officials of the party in power. In fact, these investments financed by foreign loans in large measure concern state enterprises controlled by these officials (not to mention the possibilities for parallel incomes in the form of under-the-table payments). Consequently, even in countries far removed from the state socialism exemplified, exemplified by Ghana, the public sector continued to expand with the help of foreign loans, benefiting high officials, by permitting them to pursue their careers in the sector, and especially the country's leaders, who thus can offer employment and extend their clientele. As can be seen, public investments concern many persons and powerful interests. After they had been financed domestically for several years, thanks to very favourable terms of trade, there was a great temptation to continue these investments by using foreign loans. It is also necessary to recall the responsibility of foreign banks, which supplied large sums of capital (petrodollars that they were recycling with profit) on very favourable terms for the borrowers (the real interest rates were very low, even negative, given the inflation in the industrialised countries and using their prices as a deflator).

A pertinent objection to this reasoning is that the high officials knew that such a policy could not last in the long term. Such errors could of course be explained as a sort of political myopia of leaders, who did not care about the long term since they would then no longer be in power. For a number of the countries studied, however, this explanation is not valid, because of the stability of their governments, for example, in Chile, Côte d'Ivoire, Indonesia and Morocco.

Let us note, however, that such improvident behaviour is not inevitable, for the governments of two countries, Indonesia and Malaysia, had the courage to adjust before there was a crisis. As these countries stood out in the sample by the quality of their economic management, it could be asked whether there is not a link between excellent management and the leaders' concern for the future, and whether they are not explained by one and the same phenomenon: the progress of economic rationality.

In the other countries, the cumulative process of indebtedness, persistent deterioration of the terms of trade and errors of investing in large projects that proved unproductive led to financial crisis and IMF intervention.

From that moment begin negotiations on adjustment, in which several actors take part: international organisations, the government, the civil service and pressure groups. Moreover, the affair is not over when the government and the IMF reach agreement on a stabilization programme, for the majority of these programmes are modified in course of implementation, sometimes even interrupted. Such changes are more often due to the actions of pressure groups or of the administration than by exogenous shocks that were unforeseeable during the negotiations. Obviously, the latter have a political dimension, for all programmes have major repercussions on the living standards on the various socio-economic groups, negative for some, positive for others.

The recommendations of the IMF, and those of the World Bank when stabilization is associated with a structural adjustment, always follow the same principles: reduction of the budget deficit, opening of the economy and internal liberalisation. The implementation of these principles inevitably harms several groups: public employees and persons working for the public sector, import-export merchants who benefit from protectionism, employees and heads of firms in highly protected industrial sectors. Conversely, the majority of the rural population is not unfavourably affected by adjustment measures, for devaluation benefits exporters of agricultural products and the terms of trade between the agricultural and non-agricultural sectors evolve in favour of the former. However, they can suffer from other measures which affect their standard of living, such as reduction of expenditure on education and health in rural areas. Urban groups having very low incomes — for example, persons working in the informal sector — can be hit in different ways: a decline in sales to modern sector employees or cuts in social services.

Under these conditions, the government is in a delicate situation for several reasons. The groups which have been harmed are quick to show their discontent, and they seek to have measures concerning them annulled. On the other hand, the support of groups that gain from the adjustment takes time to appear and in any case it is weak and diffuse if — as is the case — the groups are composed of widely dispersed rural dwellers. But the government can be directly threatened by hostile urban groups: public employees and wage-earners of the modern sector may go on strike, the poor who are affected by cuts in food subsidies may riot, entrepreneurs may engage in capital flight, and the bureaucracy may sabotage the implementation of the programme. Some of these things occurred in Morocco, where there were riots against increases in food prices, and in Côte d'Ivoire, where there were strikes.

Under these conditions, governments seek the support of a new coalition that favours adjustment and moderate some of stabilization measures so as not to harm the interests of those in the coalition. The government may even postpone some measures so that it does not hit too many interests at the same time. The coalition can include farmers, notably those who export, industries which look to markets abroad and those in an activity like tourism, which is linked to foreign demand. A government cannot go against the interests of the military, however, and it has need of technocrats to implement the reforms. Moreover, as much as possible it should avoid the most politically dangerous measures: sudden price rises on basic necessities owing to cuts in subsidies, and draconian restrictions on attending the university or on student grants. In fact, the desperate reactions of the poorest families or student demonstrations in the capital are difficult to control and often are highly publicised in the press abroad. Information policy should also play a role: in some countries, stabilization programmes have provoked riots and failed, simply because the government suddenly imposed harsh measures without informing the population about the financial crisis. That occurred in Santa Domingo in April 1984: riots broke out when a large devaluation and the elimination of food subsidies were introduced by surprise at the return from the Easter vacation.

The larger the coalition, the more a government is obliged to sacrifice the austerity principles of adjustment. In this respect, it is sometimes claimed that a dictatorship, which relies on a slender coalition, can carry out a stabilization programme more easily. However, the absence of multi-party elections is not necessarily an advantage for authoritarian regimes. If the majority of the population is rural and benefits from adjustment, free elections can bring support to a government. An authoritarian, but not dictatorial, government is in a more fragile situation, for it does not benefit from electoral support and yet is subject to the pressure of the urban population.

These observations show that considerations of equity often carry less weight than the balance of forces. Some measures such as cutting military expenditure, reducing the pay of public employees and a "numerus clausus" for admission to the university are very difficult to carry out, even when they are justified by efficiency and equity, for example, to avoid cutting expenditure on primary schooling or investments in rural infrastructure. The adjustment measures that we have described (Chapter I.2) are inevitably a compromise between the constraints of adjustment and the power of various interest groups. In such conditions, some equitable measures must be moderated to obtain the support of a larger coalition. For example, a subsidy on fertilizers which benefits small peasants has the advantage of also favouring large farmers who can have considerable political weight. In urban areas, a subsidy on basic food products benefits the middle class as much as — or more than — the poor, whereas aid reserved to the latter, such as food coupons, would not be supported by the middle class, especially public employees.

2. Government Capabilities and Choices

The first lesson provided by the case studies concerns the key role of statistical information, which by definition is a responsibility of the state. Donors and especially international organisations can do nothing to promote equity if they do not have the necessary statistics. Whether it is a question of knowing the composition of groups targeted for specific anti-poverty policies or using models to simulate the effects of alternative policies and choose the most equitable, nothing is possible without information, which is lacking in many countries carrying out adjustment. This negligence of statistical work is attributable to governments that do not provide the necessary resources to their statistical services, but also to international organisations and bilateral donors, which have not recognised that this expense is a necessary preliminary investment.

This negligence could also be interpreted as a political calculation, for some governments may prefer to leave their citizens in the dark about a sensitive subject like poverty or the distribution of income. However, it is a bad calculation. As we have seen, adjustment hits the urban population much more than the rural. Consequently, repercussions such as growing unemployment in the cities or widespread cases of malnutrition in the poor districts are common knowledge, despite the government's wishes. These negative effects will be denounced by the media, even in authoritarian countries; the sole exceptions are dictatorships, which manage to suppress information and impose the official truth even abroad. Thus it is better to produce and make available reliable statistics on the whole population. When that is done a government can show, for example, that the living standards of the majority of the poor did not decline, indicating the evolution of agricultural incomes and the distribution of the poor between urban and rural areas. From our case studies, it would appear that adjustment measures often have contrary effects on the poor, improving the situation of some, aggravating that of others. As news of negative examples inevitably becomes known, spread by rumour and the media, it would be better for a government to produce some complete statistics on all poor households.

The first source of information required is a national survey of household consumption, or rather successive surveys, so that there can be a comparison of the situations before and after adjustment. The examples of Indonesia and Malaysia, for which we have such surveys, reveals the importance and richness of their lessons for assessing the social consequences of adjustment. Such surveys, made every five years, would become the main instrument for following variations in average income by group and the evolution of poverty, or for estimating the effect of raising rates of public utilities or cutting subsidies. Naturally, it is necessary to use the same methodology so that the results will be comparable. The cost of such national surveys is large, but if it is absolutely necessary to reduce costs, a smaller sample could be used alternately with the main sample.

Such surveys should be rounded off by a survey of a small, constant sample of, for example, 1 000 to 1 500 households, whose characteristics are noted every one or two years. In fact, one of the lessons of this project is that adjustment has a destabilizing effect on incomes. The income pyramid is somewhat disrupted by adjustment, which suddenly accelerates movement from one income bracket to another. Many more households move up (out of poverty) or down (into poverty) than in a normal period. For example, if two successive surveys indicate the same percentage of poor, it is possible that half of the poor after adjustment had not been poor before. This mobility is explained by the positive effects of some adjustment measures (in favour of agriculture and activities linked to foreign demand) and the negative impact of others (for example, fall in construction and decline in local demand for the goods of the informal sector). Only longitudinal data obtained from a constant sample would permit a good understanding of the socio-economic effects of adjustment, so that efficacious anti-poverty policies could then be drawn up, correctly targeted on the groups hit. It is also necessary to be attentive to new forms of poverty, which can have political repercussions even if the overall level of poverty did not increase.

Obviously, it is desirable that the surveys be supplemented by other statistical sources, which can provide additional information and serve to verify certain of the results of the surveys on consumption. A very useful source would be an annual census of enterprises of the formal sector (which would include all enterprises employing more than ten persons), with detailed data on employment, wages and accounts (operating and balance sheet). This census, which exists for some of the countries studied — for example, Côte d'Ivoire and Morocco — is indispensable for determining the consequences of adjustment (whether of stabilization or structural changes) on employment and incomes in this sector, so directly and swiftly affected by adjustment. Data broken down into approximately 20 sectors will shed light on the social consequences of adjustment because these can vary from sector to sector: there can be growth in a certain exporting sector or tourism, while there is a recession in import-substitution industry or a fall in construction. If data are available only for large aggregates (like industry and construction, trade and services), it is not possible to understand the effects of adjustment. Moreover, such a census provides indirect information on the evolution of high incomes, which are always difficult to determine, through the net results of enterprises.

As the arbitrage between groups for allocating the costs of adjustment should take into account all benefits and burdens, information on the distribution of state services would be desirable. This assumes, for example, that there are statistics on families with children attending primary or secondary school or receiving higher education (socio-economic group, possibly income bracket or expenditure). The same holds for the other free services: health and sometimes housing. It is also necessary to have fiscal data to know the distribution of direct and indirect taxes by group. These statistics would permit analysts to make a balance sheet of all transfers and levies by group and to evaluate the consequences of each set of stabilization measures (new taxes, reduced food subsidies and reduced social expenditures). This information on the redistribution of income by the state, before and after adjustment, is necessary if one is to separate the effect of adjustment on primary incomes from the impact on redistribution. In negotiations between conflicting groups, each is concerned about both primary incomes and redistribution since its standard of living depends on both. If the government is concerned about transparency and equity, it must take into account all primary and secondary incomes for each group and calculate the extent to which each wins or loses.

This inventory of the statistics required for an equitable adjustment policy has not taken into account selective information needed to prepare certain measures. We mention them only as a matter of interest. For example, the preparation of a devaluation assumes some estimates of the price elasticity of foreign demand; drawing up other measures could require specialised research to quantify some parameters. It should be noted that on the whole, although a few macroeconomic data are missing, it is especially microeconomic data, like those on consumption and incomes, which will be lacking. Thus the main effort in the domain of statistics should be preparing microeconomic data bases, which will be very useful for preparing stabilization programmes and other economic policy measures.

It remains to underline the importance of statistical information in reconciling adjustment and equity. This is a requirement for efficacious action by a government in co-operation with donors, whether it is a question of targeted action or the preparation of a stabilization programme. Possession of detailed data on income and consumption by group permits rapid implementation of compensatory measures for the benefit of poor households which will experience the negative effects of adjustment. In Ghana and Morocco, such policies were able to cushion the effects of adjustment. Ghana's Programme of Action to Mitigate the Social Costs of Adjustment (PAMSCAD) was especially aimed at the victims of certain measures, such as employees of public sector and state enterprises who were laid off. In Morocco, the aid provided to mothers in poor districts and unemployed persons in rural areas benefited only the poorest; this was also true of the Chilean programme for deprived mothers and children. The more precise and detailed is the information on these groups, the less the compensatory measures will cost, since the aid will reach only the individuals concerned rather than larger groups, which include persons whose income has been stable or rising. For this reason, detailed statistical investigation is the instrument for a treatment that is at once inexpensive and efficacious. It is an indispensable instrument because the adjustment's repercussions vary greatly between groups in the working population, or from one sector to another. The adjustment's effects are neither simple nor similar for large categories of the working population or of families, contrary to what one might think because it consists of macroeconomic measures. We should point out, however, that even well-targeted aid has disadvantages. Even without sufficient information, certain governments know that some measures for assisting the poor, such as subsidies on food products and fertilizers, also benefit the middle class or even rich households, when it is a case of large farmers who buy large quantities of fertilizer. If they act in this way, it is because targeted measures could arouse political opposition (food coupons reserved to the poorest or limits on the size of farms that can purchase subsidised fertilizer). Thus the Moroccan government continues its subsidy policy to win the support of the middle classes. In countries like Ghana and Indonesia, however, the subsidies on fertilizers have been cut or ended for budgetary reasons. Thus targeting is obviously more an objective of international organisations than of governments, which must take political constraints into account.

Furthermore, this statistical information is indispensable if one wants to utilise a macro-micro model to evaluate the social consequences of alternative policies. Chapter IV showed that a large quantity of information for each socio-economic group is needed to construct a social accounting matrix and to estimate possible parameters from empirical data. The use of such a model with poor data and without information on the parameters can be hazardous because one could choose a policy based on flimsy results which none the less appear to be rigorous. Moreover, it is impossible to interpret simulations correctly if one does not have considerable knowledge of socio-economic changes during the reference period. Thus modelling work can aid in drawing up an adjustment programme, but it can never substitute for a descriptive analysis based on detailed and reliable statistics, and the quality of the aid it supplies is dependent on this basic information.

Once a government has accumulated the information necessary, an optimistic assumption, how can it best prepare the adjustment measures? Obviously, the presence of skilled groups in the administration plays an important role. In this respect, Indonesia and Malaysia are telling examples, for these two countries applied efficacious and equitable programmes that were entirely conceived by such groups, without the direct intervention of international organisations. In any case, however good their intentions, the international organisations are not experts on every country. To a certain extent, they will apply standard programmes, which may serve to reduce the main macroeconomic disequilibria but which do not take into account political constraints or considerations of equity. The role of these skilled groups is to inventory all the alternative measures in each domain, to follow and interpret trends in living standards and poverty, showing what is attributable to external shocks, adjustment measures or other factors. This information enables them to estimate the social repercussions of each measure. Finally, they can utilise a macro-micro model, like the one presented in Chapter IV, to look for the programme that can best reconcile efficacy and equity. This model usefully complements other analyses, but it does not replace them and it cannot answer all questions. In fact, it has a large grey area: it does not incorporate inequality within groups. It assumes a constant income distribution within each group from one year to another, instead of endogenising this intra-group distribution. Now, intra-group inequality represents about half the total inequality and it is affected by some measures. A simple example concerns the minimum wage policy: a revaluation of the minimum wage modifies the wage distribution within the formal sector. Surveys on incomes in Indonesia have confirmed this phenomenon: income distribution within certain groups changed significantly during the adjustment. In Morocco as well, a revaluation of the minimum wage most likely reduced wage inequalities.

In the present state of this macro-micro model the aggregates of some variables are too large. This is true of public investment. The case of Indonesia showed that it would be very useful to be able to break down this investment: the living standards of peasants increased during adjustment, because the government had been financing large investments in rural areas for about ten years. It is reasonable to assume (we have done so) that the productivity of private capital will be affected in subsequent years by public investments, but in reality, it is necessary to break down the latter into three categories:

— infrastructural investment in urban areas,

— infrastructural investment in rural areas,

— luxury or military investment.

Depending on the type of government investment, there will be different repercussions on the productivity of capital and, consequently, on incomes. To avoid these drawbacks, it would be necessary to perfect a second generation of macro-micro models for a larger number of groups and to break down aggregates more finely. If we do not have the increased data they would require, however, the development of such models would serve no purpose. Thus it is clear that progress in modelling is closely linked to that of statistical information.

When drawing up an adjustment programme one should keep its purpose in mind. Devising an ideal programme serves no purpose if the government will never be able to implement it. Given the urgency or threat of a financial crisis and the weaknesses of administrations in developing countries, it is necessary to make the best use of existing institutions rather than creating new ones which will entail cost and delay. There are two instructive examples in the study of Morocco. In 1983, this country had a network of 300 social-educational centres which served about half a million poor people. Some 65 per cent of them were in rural areas and they were located in all provinces, with a higher percentage in the most disadvantaged regions. The beneficiaries had to produce a card of indigence issued by municipal officials and their right to it was verified by a local commission. The centres gave food rations to mothers (flour, oil and powdered milk), provided instruction on nutrition and watched over children. The personnel of these centres, which have existed since the 1960s, was very experienced. With only small additional funds, the centres were able to double, or even triple, the number of beneficiaries. Furthermore, one-fourth of the children attending school in 1983 received free meals, this benefit depending on family income and size, as well as on the distance between the school and the home. Each meal provided more than half of the child's daily need in calories and proteins. With an existing organisation in place, it is easy to extend such a programme rapidly by including more beneficiaries or by adding snacks.

These two examples show how one can take advantage of existing institutions to increase transfers to the poor with very small administrative costs. A similar approach should be used when modifying taxation. In the short term, it is impossible to develop legislation and administrative services comparable to those of more developed countries. Thus it is better to use the existing fiscal system. The obstacles to progressive taxation of high incomes are well known, but doubling the fuel tax, a measure easy to apply, would have much the same effects in a country where fewer than 20 per cent of households possess an automobile. Of course, other households will also be affected because this measure will increase the cost of bus transport, but these expenses represent a rather small proportion of their budget, and some specific measures can reduce the cost of public transport to compensate for increased price of fuel.

If all these conditions are fulfilled concerning availability of statistics, skilled officials, instruments for forecasting, means of information and the like, will a government organise a dialogue among the groups concerned in order to prepare the adjustment measures in an atmosphere of co-operation and transparency?

In an ideal situation it could happen. There are even historical examples of such co-operation concerning incomes. After 1945 in several European countries, like Norway and the Netherlands, a system of consultation was established and put into practice which permitted incomes of each group to evolve in a way compatible with macroeconomic equilibria at a time when there was a risk of serious disequilibria, given the rigidity of supply in the short term and the pressure of demand resulting from the accumulation of liquid assets. Experts prepared forecasts with the aid of a model and estimated by simulation the effects of sets of alternative measures concerning incomes, taxation, public utility rates, etc. Discussion between groups and representatives of the state then focused on these policy alternatives. This method made it possible to reduce the excessive demands of certain groups and to reach compromises that the social partners agreed to respect.

Experience shows, however, that it is usually impossible to hope for such consultation in developing countries. It is often impossible even in developed countries, as the example of France shows. The European countries that we discussed above had relatively small inequalities of income, high wages and strong trade unions, to which a majority of salaried workers belonged. Moreover, these unions had close links, which they wished to sustain, with the leftist parties in power. These conditions never exist in developing countries, where conflicts of interest between groups are more serious than in developed countries and sometimes become violent.

Consequently, even if a government has all the means necessary for devising and putting into practice an equitable adjustment policy, and intends to do so, it must take into account the most powerful pressure groups. For example, the fact that public employees are paid twice the average wage of the modern sector will not convince public employees to accept a pay cut; they will react to any large loss of real income, even if they conserve their rank in the hierarchy of incomes. When there are conflicts, workers in key sectors (energy, transportation and mining) do not renounce their strategic advantage. The pressure of the middle classes in cities will prevent governments from cutting expenditure on higher education to preserve elementary education in rural areas, for these urban families are the primary beneficiaries of this expenditure and they do not have the means to finance higher education for their children. From the standpoint of their own rise in social terms, this expenditure appears more necessary than the schooling of agricultural workers' children, even if illiteracy keeps the latter in a vicious circle of poverty.

Such resistance does not preclude some stabilization measures unfavourable to the dominant interest groups. In Côte d'Ivoire, the government sharply cut expenditures on higher education, while many countries reduced the real pay of public employees and increased taxes on goods consumed by the middle classes. It was inevitable in view of the large budget deficit. Obviously, it is not possible to shift the costs of adjustment to the poorest 40 to 60 per cent, given their disadvantaged condition, the small proportion of the national income they receive and the fact that some of them live on a subsistence basis. It is incontestable, however, that governments take into account the constraints of pressure groups when they draw up stabilization programmes. That is why Indonesia cut public investment but maintained the pay of public employees, or why Chile subsidised the rich debtors owing dollars while cutting unemployment benefits.

Although constraints of pressure groups play an incontestable role, they are not the only factors determining a stabilization programme. First, a government has room to manoeuvre and is able to play one interest group against another, as in Ecuador where President Cordero had the support of rural elements, notably some exporters, against the urban middle class. Furthermore, when the programme has the support of the IMF and other donors, they often exercise pressure in favour of an equitable policy, sometimes by financing some measures favouring the poorest. Such aid is necessary since these measures entail an additional cost at the moment when the state must drastically reduce its expenditures.

Looking at our sample of countries, one observes that in no case was there a dialogue on the adjustment policy between the state and various interest groups. Moreover, such a dialogue could prove unfavourable to the poor, except in the case of Chile, where employees of the modern sector, who normally would have been a strong pressure group, especially suffered during adjustment from unemployment and large pay cuts. Indeed, the weight of the poor — agricultural workers, small peasants, the unemployed and persons working in the informal sector — is often very small.

In some cases, however, there were measures favourable to the poor: increasing social expenditures to their benefit in Malaysia, raising the minimum wage in Morocco, programmes for poor mothers and children in Chile and Morocco, aid for the most disadvantaged in Ghana (PAMSCAD), retaining food subsidies in Morocco, the programme of public works for the rural unemployed in Ecuador and the maintenance of social expenditures until 1987 in Indonesia.

How can such measures be explained when the balance of forces between pressure groups is unfavourable to the poor? There are a number of factors at work, of which the first is electoral considerations in countries where there are free elections or political alternatives, as in Malaysia or Ecuador, where President Cordero tried to keep his electoral base in rural areas by populist measures. Further, even where there is limited democracy, a government wants to avoid social protest, strikes and violent demonstrations, as in Morocco, where the food subsidies could no longer be put in question after the troubles of 1981. Moreover, even a dictatorial regime as in Chile, which did not rely on popular support, was concerned about its image abroad. A rapid decrease in infant mortality and a drop in malnutrition constituted arguments against foreign critics. Finally, international organisations and donors have insisted that the social costs of adjustment be cushioned and have financed programmes like PAMSCAD in Ghana.

Thus experience shows that governments have a margin for manoeuvre despite the weight of pressure groups that often represent the urban middle and wealthy classes. This margin could be widened by institutional reforms giving more weight to the electorate in rural areas, where a majority of the poor live (except in a country like Chile), or through more forceful action by international organisations and donors, based on aid. Indeed, even if the choice of a more equitable but equally effective stabilization programme does not entail additional costs, some compensatory measures for the poor may represent a cost difficult to bear in a budget crisis, thus foreign assistance can be justified.

3. Choices in Stabilization

The announcement of a stabilization often provokes a rejection of stabilization. That is the reaction of opposition parties, which accuse the government of giving in to the demands of the IMF, even though other solutions are possible and preferable. It is indispensable to dispel this myth. Actually, a rejection of stabilization can correspond to three different situations. The first, which is mentioned only for the record, is that of a country which avoids the constraints of stabilization because of politically motivated aid. The normal sources of financing having been exhausted, the country can no longer borrow from commercial banks without first obtaining an IMF loan. For political reasons, however, a certain country agrees to accord new loans or even provide gifts. Thanks to this practice, it is possible for investment and growth to continue, for there to be income gains for each group and for poverty and unemployment to decline. As the external deficits get worse, the indebtedness reaches the point where even this lender refuses new loans or considers further transfers as gifts. It is evident that no stabilization programme, however equitable, could bear comparison with the advantages of unconditional aid. It remains to mention the political price, for such aid has its counterpart, for example, in providing access to military bases or votes in international organisations. Moreover, only a small country can be in this position, otherwise, a "lender" could not support this financial cost for long.

The second, more classic situation involves a country which refuses to negotiate with IMF and decides to ration imports. This leads to a sort of "forced" adjustment, for imports are compressed to such a point that the country can use its balance-of-trade surplus to repay its debts and stop borrowing. Another variant consists of repudiating the debt and adjusting imports to export receipts. This strategy automatically converts the economy to "self-centred" development, a model often proposed by the most hard-line opponents of any adjustment programme. That was just what Ghana did, and we have been able to measure its very heavy costs: fall of per capita income, of commercial crops, of exports, of imports, of real wages and of peasant incomes. Consequently, the number of poor and the intensity of poverty both increased. The Ghanaian experience, and that of other countries which took a similar path, confirms the macro-micro model's forecasts of a simulation of not adjusting in Morocco. Rationing permits putting a quick end to the deficit in the current account, but at a high cost: fall in per capita income, fall in industrial production and investment linked directly to the rationing, and a large increase in poverty. Moreover, the rationing provides traders with rents, leading to an increase in inequality. Marketing controls on imported goods can prevent this indirect effect, but experience shows that this leads to the development of a parallel market with other disadvantages and abuses. As can be seen, this strategy merits the appellation of "self-centred recession". It is necessary to refer to these experiences of not adjusting because of the systematic criticism of all stabilization programmes. In this respect, it would be desirable to study other countries which followed the same policy as Ghana, for this would permit listing the effects common to all these experiences of non-adjustment. It would be possible to shift the basis of political discussion of adjustment, if it were clearly shown that this strategy always has high economic and social costs. Such discussion is misleading when the comparison lists the costs of adjustment but ignores the higher costs of not adjusting. Such studies and their distribution would acquaint public opinion with the advantages and disadvantages of each solution.

The third situation, illustrated by the study of Ecuador, is a special case. Actually, it was an adjustment which used the single instrument of devaluation. It is assumed that the country has a floating exchange rate which automatically adjusted to balance the current account. Moreover, the government takes no budgetary or monetary measures to reduce the macroeconomic disequilibria. Devaluation can be an efficacious and equitable instrument when used with other stabilization measures, but when used alone it has disadvantages: increased inflation (unless the growth of the money supply is strictly controlled), increased interest rates, which slow investment, and finally, capital flight if new devaluations are expected. The yield of each stabilization measure declines with the intensification of its use. Consequently, a floating exchange rate unaccompanied by other measures could not be more advantageous than a well-chosen combination of stabilization measures.

As soon as there is a decision to stabilize, two questions merit special attention: the choice of timing and the external shocks. Timing is fundamental because it influences the stabilization programme. As we have seen, it is possible to stabilize before, during and even after the financial crisis, as Ghana did. The examples of Malaysia and Indonesia revealed the advantages of anticipating the crisis. Politically, the government is not obliged to negotiate with the IMF and, in effect, recognise its errors of management. This prevents neither consultations with the IMF and World Bank nor loans for structural reform, but if it acts before a crisis the government is in a better position for discussions with these two organisations and for getting its stabilization plan accepted by public opinion. Economically, this plan inevitably has costs in growth and investment, their impact only being postponed, but they are also somewhat lessened because the disequilibria to be absorbed are smaller. Consequently, the social costs in unemployment and poverty are also lessened. These result from a simulated anticipated adjustment in Morocco (in 1981 instead of 1983), are confirmed by the experiences of Indonesia and Malaysia. These two countries which stabilized before the crisis were better able to reconcile adjustment and equity than the other countries. This success is partly linked to the timing. For example, Malaysia increased per capita expenditure on education and health during the adjustment. If adjustment had been postponed a few years, it would have been necessary to cut public expenditures more sharply and it would thus have been impossible to safeguard the social expenditures. Moreover, as the recession would have been much more serious, employment would have fallen and real wages would have declined, while in reality they still increased by 9 per cent between 1983 and 1987.

An early adjustment has the important advantage of guaranteeing a large and continued flow of external capital before and during the adjustment period, from which Malaysia and especially Indonesia benefited. This attenuates the reduction of public expenditure, or even permits it to increase, and also avoids a fall in private investment. These advantages have some fundamental social consequences: drastic cuts in social expenditures are avoided and continued investment has direct effects on employment in construction, which employs low-skilled labour. On the other hand, when a country delays adjustment as long as possible, the flow of foreign capital ceases for several years before an IMF loan is obtained, with unfavourable social consequences.

Another advantage of early adjustment is that it gives the government room to manoeuvre. In a crisis, a government can no longer delay putting into effect a stabilization programme regardless of the international economic situation or the uncertainties in weather conditions. It is known that developing countries are subject to these risks, for international prices of agricultural and mineral products fluctuate much more than prices of manufactured goods exported by industrialised countries. Agriculture, which often supports more than half of a developing country's population and provides a good proportion of its exports, is directly dependent on the weather. Consequently, in case of a financial crisis, not being able to postpone a stabilization programme, even for a year, is a great disadvantage when the country is also suffering from an external shock.

Actually, it is astonishing that governments wait so long to act despite the advantages of acting earlier. This can only be result of myopia or unfulfilled expectations. In the short term, two or three years, it is obvious that increased indebtedness has all the advantages and permits gains in income, transfers and employment for all groups. On the other hand, in countries where political power changes regularly, a government could gamble on leaving the thankless task of stabilization to its successor. While waiting out these two or three years, however, the government loses an important political argument, that of having minimised the costs of adjustment.

Various factors can lead to delaying adjustment. First, there is a period of learning, for public opinion begins by preferring the advantages of indebtedness to the costs of adjustment. With the passage of time, the inconveniences of macroeconomic disequilibria become increasingly apparent, and a programme that was initially rejected can become acceptable to the majority, who have understood that in time adjustment is inevitable. Political instability, under either a democratic or an authoritarian system, can compromise the will to act because the government assumes it will be out of power by the time the financial crisis breaks out. Per capita income also plays a role, for the poorer a country is, the more the costs of adjustment appear to be unbearable and the less qualified the administration will be to implement structural reforms efficiently. Finally, constitutional provisions, such as a requirement that there be a balanced budget, can make it more difficult to delay an adjustment, as was seen in Indonesia. Conversely, some practices promote delay: for example, generalised indexation, which prevents groups from feeling the effects of inflation, or a sort of veto accorded to some groups. Thus public employees, enjoying an unrestricted right to strike, can prevent a government supported by a democratic majority from undertaking a stabilization programme which plans a sharp reduction in the pay of public employees and workers in the public sector (transportation and energy). Even if this measure were completely justified, a paralysis of the administration and public utilities could block governmental action. Such points of blockage can also exist outside the administration. For example, employees of key sectors have a right of veto out of proportion to their electoral weight: workers in energy, transportation or mining in a country whose foreign currency receipts come entirely from mineral exports. To avoid delaying adjustment in such circumstances, it is necessary to accept the privileged status of such workers, that is, exempt them from sharing the costs of stabilization.

These examples show that a variety of steps should be undertaken to struggle against delaying factors. Institutions guaranteeing government stability can constrain a government which must face an election, for example, every two years. A five-year presidential system or a parliamentary system in which the government is linked to the majority, also for five years, provide efficacious means. Respect for democracy is compatible with institutions permitting a government to remain in office for long periods. It should also lead to constitutional provisions which prohibit public employees from paralysing a government supported by a majority of the electorate. As has been mentioned, other constitutional provisions, such as the requirement of a balanced budget, can be useful controls, providing the government with better means of resisting pressures of different groups. These examples show that the reform of political institutions can be a determining factor favouring early adjustment, which is the least costly from all points of view. A government itself should act in the same manner. For example, it can give more independence to the central bank or modify budget procedures to avoid excesses.

When an economy starts running out of control, the authorities might try to hide the fact from public opinion or to minimise its importance, fearing that it would be seen as a sign of failure of their policies. A government might sometimes be correct in hoping that trends could be reversed by an unknown in the international situation — for example, a rapid improvement of the terms of trade — but this practice is dangerous because it anaesthetizes public opinion. Public opinion should be alerted and prepared for stabilization measures by the publication of annual or semi-annual reports on the state of the economy, made widely available to the media, indicating the development of disequilibria and their consequences. Given the cost and expertise needed for such research, a single regional body could be envisaged to survey the economies of several small countries.

This picture of the advantages of adjustment before a crisis and of the factors promoting delay raises this question: Why did some countries of sample, Indonesia and Malaysia, adjust before a crisis but not the others? First, we will exclude the case of Ghana, whose government rejected any adjustment policy for reasons of socialist ideology in the 1970s. Concerning Morocco, it should be recalled that before the 1983 programme, attempts in 1979 and 1981 failed because of domestic opposition and unfavourable external factors. In Côte d'Ivoire, a role was played by the hope for an improvement of the terms of trade which would facilitate the reimbursement of the debt. Finally, the financial situation of the countries would have made an independent adjustment policy difficult. For example, Ecuador undertook some stabilization measures beginning in 1982, but it went to the IMF in 1983 because its situation was not as solid as that of Indonesia and Malaysia. Thus it appears that the government's attitude is not the only explanatory factor, because the possibilities for independent adjustment before a crisis vary widely according to domestic and international conditions.

In addition to the timing, it appears that stabilization programmes often neglect to take into account external shocks. When a programme is negotiated with the IMF, annual or quarterly goals are fixed for key indicators, and the release of successive credit tranches is linked to performance based on the indicators. In view of the importance of uncertainties confronting developing economies, however, it is desirable to plan for some complementary contingency financing. The provision of these funds would depend on the nature and extent of possible calamities, such as an earthquake, drought or decline of the terms of trade. For example, variable compensation could be envisaged, depending on whether the fall in terms of trade is between 10 and 20 per cent, between 20 and 30 per cent, or even more. As this is a matter of pure loss for a country, the compensation should be in the form of grants by industrialised countries. When there a deterioration of the terms of trade or an increase in interest rate, it is clear that the industrialised countries, as a whole, benefit from the shocks. When it a matter of a natural calamity, like an earthquake or drought, these countries serve as insurers who provide compensation for damages without having received premiums. In the case of some calamities, developing countries can be held responsible for their misfortune, for example, excessive output of a certain export crop could itself contribute to the decline in the terms of trade. However, it is possible to envisage restrictive covenants that would avoid this type of snag.

The example of Morocco reveals the importance of these exogenous shocks. According to a simulation with the macro-micro model, the drought of 1981 increased the current account deficit by 25 per cent, reduced household consumption by 5 per cent and increased the intensity of poverty by 16 per cent. This example is especially interesting because Morocco should have undertaken a stabilization programme in 1980 or 1981, given the increased disequilibria at the end of the 1970s. Without external compensation, the combination of a stabilization programme and drought in 1981 would have had very grave social consequences, for the former sharply augmented urban poverty in 1983-84 and the latter, rural poverty in 1981. A combination of the two would have led to a general increase in poverty in the whole country. Furthermore, this crisis would have some cumulative effects. For example, persons active in the informal sector in major cities suffered income losses following a drop in demand, but in smaller cities and villages they benefited from the rapid growth of agricultural incomes beginning in 1985. If there had been a drought during the second year of the stabilization programme all persons active in the informal sector would have been hit at the same time, with a multiplier effect because internal relations in this sector are highly developed (inputs purchased from other informal enterprises, expenditures on consumption goods and services of the informal sector). These risks do not imply that there should not have been a stabilization beginning in 1980, but they show that foreign grants would have had to compensate for the 1981 drought. Such grants could have been targeted, for example, by distribution of grain to poor peasants.

Having considered the decision to stabilize and steps to insure against external shocks, we have reached the main objective of this project: how to minimise the social costs of stabilization. As was seen in Chapter IV, several macro-micro models have been constructed, each with its specificities, though all are based on the same principles; they were applied to different economies, so their structural parameters are more or less far apart; and the authors of the different studies did not follow a strictly uniform procedure in the simulations. Despite all these elements of diversity, some constants emerged from the five countries modeled; some stabilization measures always had unfavourable effects, others favourable ones. Obviously, one must avoid the mistake of assuming that because a measure ranked highest in its effects it can be used as the sole adjustment measure, for that would involve the risk of decreasing yields. For example, if a moderate reduction in the pay of public employees (of -20 per cent) has more favourable effects on the social indicators (unemployment rate, inequality, number of poor and intensity of poverty) than other measures do, it would be absurd to assume that these wages should be cut by 60 per cent, to the exclusion of other measures. A cut of 60 per cent would give rise to negative effects: some low-paid public employees would fall below the poverty line, there would be a general refusal to work for the administration and the quality of public services would plummet. This example shows that effects are not proportional to the application of measures and that a ranking should guide the choice of an optimal combination of measures, but not of one alone.

That said, it is nonetheless seen that some measures should be avoided, while others should be given preference. Two measures always had highly negative effects: increasing indirect taxation and laying off public employees to reduce public expenditures.

Some simulations on Morocco, comparing eight measures which produced the same reduction in the budget deficit, showed that the increase in indirect taxes is the most harmful not only in social terms — it produces the greatest increases in unemployment and poverty — but also in economic terms, as it leads to the largest decline in GDP. Simulations for two other countries, Côte d'Ivoire and Malaysia, led to the same conclusion. The poor are directly hit by price rises (it was assumed that the same tax rate was applied to all goods), and this rise reduces expenditures of persons active in the formal sector, which in turn leads to lower prices and incomes in the informal sector, where many of the poor work. This contraction of demand also explains a swelling of unemployment in the formal sector. Lay-offs of public employees also have highly negative effects. On the one hand, they directly increase unemployment and the number of persons active in the informal sector and, as a result, lead to a decline in average income of these persons (since adjustment between supply and demand is made by prices, the supply being proportional to the number of persons active in the informal sector). On the other hand, these lay-offs immediately reduce educational, health or other services for households, which lowers the living standards of the poor.

At the other end of our ranking are two measures whose social impact is more favourable, or less unfavourable, than those of the other measures: a devaluation and a moderate decrease in the pay of public employees. In the aforementioned comparison of eight measures in Morocco, a devaluation is the least costly in terms of growth, unemployment and poverty. Furthermore, it reduces inequality of incomes. This simulation, like those for other countries, shows that devaluation favours the farmers who export at the expense of persons employed in the modern sector. In fact, the prices of exported agricultural products rise while the real pay of public employees decreases as a result of higher inflation. This decrease rests on the assumption that the pay is only partially indexed to the cost of living. As farmers have more resources they spend more, which benefits the informal sector (they devote a higher proportion of expenditures to goods from this sector than other households do). Consequently, this increase in demand compensates for a decline in demand in urban areas, and the average income of persons active in the informal sector is less affected by devaluation than by other measures. Moreover, devaluation entails an increase in the cost of living that increases with income and that, for equal incomes, is greater in cities than in rural areas because the share of imported goods in consumption increases with income and urbanisation. These divergent trends in the real incomes of persons working in the modern sector, agriculture and the informal sector mean that devaluation reduces inequality without increasing poverty.

This optimistic assessment should be qualified, for several reasons. If export-oriented agriculture is concentrated in the hands of big farmers, as in Ecuador and other Latin American countries, an increase in agricultural prices does not benefit the small farmers and there is no decrease in rural poverty. Moreover, a devaluation leads to an increase in inflation if the growth of the money supply is not strictly controlled, and consequently to a rise in the nominal interest rate. If the economy enters an inflationary spiral, it will be necessary to devalue again and the economic agents will modify their expectations. Workers will demand a complete indexation of their wages, while entrepreneurs will invest their capital abroad and borrow domestic funds, speculating on further inflation. In light of these risks, devaluation is desirable only if the small and medium farmers export part of their output (and/or if it stimulates labour-intensive export industries). Thus devaluation is a good measure only if it is accompanied by other stabilization measures and, as was shown above, a policy consisting only of a floating exchange rate is not the solution to the crisis.

A moderate decrease in the wages of public employees is also a desirable measure. In view of their place in the hierarchy of incomes, it lessens income inequality and does not have a large effect on poverty. Moreover, it appears to be the least costly for growth: a comparison for Morocco of four means of reducing public expenditure and the foreign deficit (reducing the number of employees, average wages, public investment and current expenditure, excluding wages), shows it to be the most favourable measure for growth, unemployment, investment and inequality. Comparable simulations for Côte d'Ivoire lead to the same conclusion. Also a simulation on Indonesia, in which wages were cut by 20 per cent to benefit public investment (+27 per cent) with an unchanged budget, showed that growth picked up after three or four years and that there were gains by agricultural workers, small and medium farmers, and the urban and rural poor, while groups with high incomes lost. Of course, as shown above, an excessive cut would have negative economic and social effects, but that is not true for the simulated cuts, which range from 10 to 20 per cent and represent one of the recommended measures for a stabilization programme. For political reasons, however, there must not be cuts in nominal wages; the decrease should result from inflation. It is also possible to lessen hostile reactions by employing youth at the minimum wage for public works programmes, these hirings compensating to some extent for the wage policy. However, implementing this measure poses an obvious political problem. The influence of public employees is disproportionate to their number, and they could effectively intervene from the moment the programme was being prepared to block a measure which affects them. Moreover, they have various means of jeopardizing the implementation of a programme: by strikes in key sectors which paralyse the economy and cause large losses in relation to the wages at stake, for example, in state enterprises (transportation, energy), and by political criticism, taken up by the media, which they can do more easily than other groups because of their concentration in the capital and links between certain public employees — for example, teachers — and the press. There is an evident contrast with the position of another group, construction workers and builders in rural areas. It the state cuts public investment in rural areas and sharply reduces incomes of these workers and entrepreneurs, there is no reaction because they are dispersed and, for the most part, poor and without the means of reacting. This example shows that some measures involve a sharp contradiction between the objective of equity and its political feasibility.

In countries where there is high unemployment of young people in cities that risks being increased by the stabilization programme, it would perhaps be desirable to link these wage decreases with the hiring of unemployed young persons, provided that it is done outside the wage-scale of public employees, that is, at a much lower rate. This is all the more necessary as the wages of minor public employees are often higher than those they would receive in the private sector, while the converse is true for high-level public employees. This labour could be used for works which would have a direct impact on the living standards of the poor: construction of roads, improvements in shanty towns, etc. This would reduce poverty while combating unemployment and improving the living standards of the poor households in urban areas. Moreover, it does not have any long-term consequences for public employees. As the wages are very low, many of these young persons will leave the jobs when enterprises begin hiring again when economic activity picks up.

Apart from cutting its employees' wages, the state can reduce public expenditure in two ways: cuts in public investment or current expenditure. As was seen in Chapter I, a stabilization policy usually has the greatest effect on investment, but this observation is biased because investment during adjustment is compared with investment in the years immediately before. Often the 1970s had been marked by an investment boom as a result of large price increases of the products exported. Except for petroleum, these increases did not last very long, and the primary cause of disequilibria and indebtedness at the beginning of the 1980s was the continuation of large investments by the state. Consequently, it would be more correct to determine the decline in investments by a comparison with their level before the 1974-80 boom. When this is done, the decline appears much smaller and in some instances there was none, but trends still varied greatly from country to country: for example, public investment was reduced much less in Indonesia and Malaysia than in Côte d'Ivoire and Morocco. The arbitrage in budget cuts between investment and other expenditure also varied depending on the country. Thus it would be useful to estimate the short- to medium-term economic and social consequences of this decision.

Compared with other budget measures, the reduction of investment is always distinguished by two obvious characteristics: greater reductions in total investment (public plus private) and in imports (given the high level of imported goods in investment). Furthermore, the cost in growth is greater than that of a devaluation or a reduction of pay of public employees. Finally, the simulations for several countries reveal the same short-term social effects: inequality and poverty increases, because about half of investment expenditures are for construction and public works, domains which make intensive use of low-skilled workers. Moreover, this measure has negative effects (lower growth of per capita income) in the medium to long term, since the productivity of private investment depends on state-financed infrastructural investment. These effects are aggravated if the cuts in public investment affect rural areas. In fact, increases in productivity and incomes of small peasants are highly dependent on this investment, as proven in the case of Indonesia, where such increases occurred during the adjustment period as a result of investments made in the 1970s. Consequently, cuts in these investments have strongly negative effects on poverty and inequality in the medium to long term.

Is this rather negative assessment a condemnation of the policies of all the countries studied? An answer should be qualified for several reasons. First, there is a problem of reference: if over a ten-year period there had been a four-fold increase in a state's public investments while its current expenditure had doubled, a 50 per cent cut in capital outlays would bring their growth in line with other expenditures. A number of the countries experienced this sort of distortion in public expenditure before adjustment, a distortion unsustainable in the long run. Furthermore, in some countries these investments were not very productive. The marginal coefficient of capital increased to the extent that the state continued making inefficient investments financed by foreign loans. In light of this rapid growth of investment and the errors committed, it was necessary to put the house in order. Moreover, some political factors and external constraints were involved. We have already explained why it is much easier for a government to cut expenditure for public works than to reduce the pay of public employees. In addition, after the financial crisis developed, the foreign banks which had financed part of the projects became very prudent. Even if a country strictly applied the programme drawn up with the IMF, it became difficult to obtain loans from these banks for new investments by state industrial and transportation enterprises. The difficulty is all the greater because these enterprises are often in a disastrous financial state and are responsible for a large proportion of the foreign debt. Policies carried out since 1974 explain and justify the drastic cuts in public investment in countries like Côte d'Ivoire and Morocco. These cuts were much less serious in countries which did not commit certain errors. We can draw two conclusions from this historical approach. Severe cuts are inevitable when public investments have grown rapidly and have been poorly managed. Yet even in this case, as in countries experiencing moderate cuts, investments in rural areas which, in the medium run, benefit the poor and middle farmers should not be trimmed. For two reasons, stabilization programmes should not touch these infrastructure investments: to prevent an immediate aggravation of poverty in rural areas owing to a drop in incomes and employment in the non-agricultural sector, and to permit a future reduction in poverty through increased incomes of small peasants.

According to the simulations, reductions in current expenditure appear preferable to cutting investments because their immediate consequences — a decline in national income and total investment, an increase in unemployment and poverty — are less serious. Furthermore, in the medium term (three to five years), there is higher growth of national output because the productivity of private sector capital is not affected by a cut in public investment. Thus it is desirable to include cuts in current expenditures (excluding wages) in a stabilization programme. If negative social consequences are to be avoided, however, cuts should depend on the category and those with social purposes should be exempted. In fact, experience shows that cuts in education and especially health expenditures hit poor families. For example, following budget cuts, hospitals can institute charges for medications which can prevent the poor from obtaining hospital care, even if equipment and care are free. Furthermore, cuts applied bureaucratically in a poor economy can have catastrophic consequences: many hospital services could be paralysed by a temporary shortage of some product. It is preferable to reduce current expenditure of the administration or the military. Living standards of populations are not affected by a reduction of military exercises or of official travelling of public employees.

These considerations on an ideal schema for reducing public expenditure nonetheless err by a lack of realism. First, some countries face threats to their independence from neighbours and there are frequent nationalist conflicts in young, independent nations, which can justify large military budgets in relation to national resources. Above all, governmental freedom of choice is in all cases limited by pressure groups: the military, public employees, workers in key sectors, wealthy entrepreneurs and even students. When public expenditure must be reduced, the resulting arbitrage is explained by the interplay of pressure groups. For example, expenditure on elementary schooling in rural areas could be cut because it was not possible to impose a *numerus clausus* on university enrolment. Similarly, public investments in rural areas might be eliminated to the detriment of peasants and small construction enterprises, while an investment project being carried out by a large enterprise whose owner is close to the government is left intact. Even though the pay of public employees is considerably higher than in the private sector, a restructuring to reduce these wages and to employ unemployed youth is avoided. It is difficult for a government to resist pressures in the context of an increasingly fragile economy, with mounting unemployment, growing poverty and accumulation of discontent. In this situation, international organisations should help governments carry out measures which it cannot implement alone, by making them conditions of new loans. Such intervention can be consistent with the goal of equity because the most disadvantaged — small peasants, agricultural workers, unemployed youth and workers in the urban informal sector — have no means of pressuring governments and because budget cuts desired by pressure groups risk hitting the poor first.

At the end of this examination of stabilization measures, it is still necessary to consider monetary policy. It could be left to the end because of its neutrality: all simulations of monetary policy, whether they are more or less rigorous than those used during adjustment, reveal a certain neutrality. For example, a tighter monetary policy reduces the average income of each group in nearly the same proportion and does not modify inequality. However, this means that poverty increases since poor households are affected like the others, which is not the case with a devaluation, assuming that small farmers export agricultural products. On the other hand, this monetary policy should be accompanied by a stabilization of nominal wages of public employees, which progressively reduces their real pay.

This point underlines an important effect of monetary policy, namely, the control of inflation, which has consequences on the distribution of property. In fact, the majority of the poor in cities have only money, while rich households in both rural areas and cities mainly have real assets: land, homes, buildings and machinery. In particular, they often keep some of their liquid assets abroad or in foreign currency. Consequently, poor household are hit more by the currency devaluation due to inflation. Thus by stimulating inflation, devaluation increases inequality of the distribution of property while it is decreased by a tight monetary policy.

As we have seen in these considerations on the social consequences of stabilization measures, all programmes should consist of a set of measures. The comparison of their social effects led to an exclusion of all increases in indirect taxation and lay-offs of public employees. On the other hand, it is desirable to combine a decrease in the pay of public employees with a devaluation and a tight monetary policy. This combination could be rounded off by a reduction of current expenditure, provided social expenditures are not touched, and of public investment, if before adjustment it had been rapidly expanded and poorly managed. However, investments in rural infrastructure should be retained.

These choices, guided by a concern for equity, go against the interests of certain groups, who will exercise pressure to go further in some areas, less far in others. Most stabilization programmes contain a common set of measures, but the political arbitrages dictated by special interests lead to weighting these measures differently. It is obvious that public employees are hostile to pay cuts. A large devaluation will incite strong opposition from the urban population, especially of the middle and upper classes, given the composition of their consumption. If public investment is cut, investment in rural areas risks being sacrificed first because its immediate beneficiaries (workers and small builders) and in the end, farmers have much less influence than urban populations who favour the infrastructure they use. Moreover, the interest of some political figures and public employees lies in preserving large industrial projects, which enhance their power, enable them to offer jobs or provide hidden income for decision makers. None of these advantages accrue to persons close to the government from rural infrastructure projects which reduce poverty. Moreover, it is easier for a government to cut current expenditures on education or health than those for national defense in countries where the regime's stability is precarious.

Even if a government could make a choice based entirely on equity, there exist conflicts of interest among the poor. Those who live in cities work mainly in the informal sector; a decline in wages of public employees reduces demand and hence incomes in this sector, while it has no effect on the conditions of the rural poor. Moreover, it is in the interest of the urban poor that cuts in expenditure on urban infrastructure be less than those for rural infrastructure. If cuts in current expenditure touch food subsidies, poor urban households and peasants who sell subsidised products will suffer, but self-sufficient peasants will not.

A government which wishes to minimise the social costs of adjustment should mix stabilization measures according to their different effects, but it also can intervene directly, paying compensation to the poor hit by the stabilization programme. The amount would correspond to the variation of the poverty gap, that is, the sum of the income that would be needed for all the poor to reach the poverty threshold. This payment compensates for the growth of poverty and stabilizes it at the pre-adjustment level. In the case of Morocco, with the aid of the macro-micro model the payment has been estimated to be 1.5 per cent of the total income of households. Although this appears to be modest, it is not negligible in budgetary terms since it is about 5 per cent of public expenditure. In other countries, however, this payment would be much larger (4 per cent of household income in Ecuador). The financing of this payment would pose a problem in the framework of a stabilization programme which requires a rapid reduction of expenditure and of the deficit. Additional cuts in investments or current expenditure would slow growth. The two solutions which avoid this problem would be an income tax on large incomes or external aid. The first possibility would involve a delay, like all structural reforms, and it would provoke political opposition since the high-income group is already affected by other stabilization measures. Furthermore, high-income households could react by placing their capital abroad, even by leaving the country (those who have higher education degrees would most easily find work in developed countries). It would thus be politically more feasible to use foreign aid, especially since it would be limited to two or three years.

None of the countries in the sample used such monetary transfers (which, in any case, would have not been justified in a country like Indonesia where poverty declined during the adjustment) but countries like Chile and Morocco continued or increased in-kind transfers to benefit the poorest: free meals in elementary schools for children of poor districts and food for mothers from poor families, which was distributed in social centres that also checked the health of mothers and children. A decline in the rate of infant mortality and the level of malnutrition in Chile despite the fall in monetary income of the poor families proves the efficacy of such a programme. It also presents the advantage of having low administrative costs and avoiding losses since the aid is targeted. These countries probably could have, in large measure, compensated for the increase in poverty entailed by the stabilization programme, by extending the aforementioned measures to more beneficiaries and adding other steps, like the hiring of unemployed youth to work on infrastructure, renewal and the like in rural areas and in poor urban districts. Thus it appears likely that a policy of compensation is possible, provided that it has external financing. It is also possible to link stabilization and compensation measures. If the principles of compensation and a fixed level of external aid were part of all programmes, a government could adapt the measures to minimise the impact of stabilization on poverty, since all transfers exceeding the aid must be financed by the national budget.

4. The Choices in Structural Adjustment

The framework for these choices is different, for the effects of structural adjustment measures can be seen only after several years — at least three or four, and sometimes ten — and their effects are permanent, while stabilization measures act in the short term and, except in case of failure, should cease after three or four years.

In principle, groups defend their interests much less vigorously when they are reacting to measures whose effects will be felt in five years rather than three months. Moreover, some structural measures appear to be neutral, like financial liberalisation or administrative reform. A structural adjustment programme takes longer to implement than a stabilization programme and entails less acute conflicts than does an immediate reduction in total demand obtained by cutting a certain public expenditure.

It must be recognised, however, that certain issues inevitably are sources of conflict. A decision to cut customs duties from 200 to 40 per cent within the space of two or three years threatens the profits and even the existence of overprotected, inefficient enterprises. Raising producer prices in agriculture and liberalisation of these prices have an immediate effect on farmers' incomes. A reform of the public sector involving thousands of lay-offs is important to the workers of this sector. These examples show that some structural adjustment measures are not neutral and can cause conflict. Moreover, the relative significance of these measures varies greatly from country to country, whereas stabilization programmes all contain the same standard measures.

Thus it is useful to recall the social consequences of the most frequently used measures before seeing how a structural adjustment programme should be adapted for considerations of equity.

As seen in Chapter I, structural adjustment programmes are inspired by the common principle of liberalising domestic and foreign trade. A review of the diverse measures in different countries shows that, directly or indirectly, many have the same objective of increasing the role of market forces.

An analysis of these measures shows that liberalisation is ordinarily compatible with equity. In agriculture, structural adjustment aims at restoring truth in pricing, for example, by ending subsidies on fertilizers, raising the cost of water and increasing producer prices. Moreover, since there often are monopolies supplying inputs and marketing products, competition is restored by permitting private enterprises to function in these markets. The results of this truth-in-pricing operation are ordinarily favourable. In general, controls on producer prices of export crops have been a means of appropriating a surplus from agriculture to finance investments in the non-agricultural sector (even for a state's current expenditure). Consequently, farmers benefit from an increase in the official price or a liberalisation of agricultural prices. Except when export crops are entirely in the hands of big farmers as in Ecuador, these price changes diminish the gap between average agricultural and average non-agricultural income and also lead to a decrease in poverty because most of the poor live in rural areas. However, this is not true if adjustment increases only the prices of inputs. This occurred in Indonesia, where fertilizer subsidies were reduced without changing the price system which was already free. In this case, there had been a transfer from the non-agricultural to the agricultural sector before adjustment. Truth in pricing is favourable to farmers in a majority of countries because the state has effected, through its system of controls and subsidies, a transfer in the opposition direction, from the agricultural to the non-agricultural sector. Moreover, farmers ordinarily benefit from the abolition of monopolies accorded to state enterprises because the latter's inefficiency. In fact, they overcharge for their services. For example, in Ghana cocoa producers financed the Cocobod, which had a monopoly on collecting and exporting cocoa. In 20 years, the Cocobod's employees increased from 5 000 to 100 000, although the body's tasks had halved since the amount being marketed had fallen in that proportion. During the adjustment, the producer price of cocoa was increased seven-fold from 1983 to 1987, approaching the price on the international market, while part of the Cocobod's activities have been privatised and nearly half of its personnel have been laid off. These lay-offs created a social problem but put an end to unjustifiable levies on the incomes of planters.

In the non-agricultural sector, adjustment involves the abolition of price controls, when they exist. In countries like Ghana, official prices had little relation to free prices and many goods were rationed. A parallel market had developed, however, where the same manufactured goods were available at much higher prices. In this case, liberalisation resulted in employment losses since the numerous small merchants of the parallel market no longer served any need. In this case as with the Cocobod's lay-offs, liberalisation had a dual effect of raising the real incomes of a large number of households (planters, urban population) and abolishing the livelihoods of certain groups. These lost livelihoods involve some tens of thousands of persons, and it will take years before they can find employment, even if liberalisation leads to economic recovery. In this situation, it is obvious that the compensation programme financed by the World Bank and other donors is indispensable since liberalisation has taken away all means of existence from some groups.

Fortunately, other adjustment measures do not exhibit such drawbacks. As the cost of capital is often underestimated, various measures seek to increase it, like fiscal amortization on less favourable terms, raising interest rates, etc. As the cost of capital with respect to labour increases, labour-intensive activities are stimulated, thus diminishing unemployment and, consequently, poverty.

The liberalisation of foreign trade is the second facet of structural adjustment, and often the most important. On the one hand, this liberalisation is aimed at opening the economy by abolishing all quotas and reducing customs duties to a moderate level (40 per cent), and on the other hand, at promoting exports by abolishing barriers such as export duties and licenses. This policy of shifting the economy towards external outlets is also based on devaluation, which is both a structural adjustment and stabilization measure. Some special measures can round off this arrangement, for example, authorising enterprises which produce for export to import intermediate products without limit or duty, as in Indonesia. In Chile, the World Bank financed a forestry programme and aided other non-mining exports.

We next consider the social consequences of these two aspects of liberalisation of foreign trade. The abolition of quotas and reduction of customs duties on imported manufactured goods affects workers and entrepreneurs of overprotected and inefficient enterprises. A survey in Morocco revealed that they were only a small minority. Nevertheless they exist. If the enterprise survives, there is a marked drop in wages and profits, but this decline does not increase inequality or poverty, given the place in the income hierarchy of workers of the protected sector. On the other hand, when there is bankruptcy and unemployment, a rapid expansion of the exporting industries is indispensable to providing jobs for the unemployed. Yet the most important phenomenon is the downward pressure on prices of manufactured goods, a decline which improves, to the farmers' benefit, the terms of trade between the agricultural and non-agricultural sectors. Consequently, in all countries where the majority of the poor are small peasants, this decline reduces poverty by increasing purchasing power. These conclusion proved *a contrario* by the negative social consequences of protectionism. A study of some 20 countries has shown that, other things being equal, a protectionist policy markedly increased inequality (the inequality indicator increases by 10 per cent) and decreased the share of the poorest 60 per cent in the national income (a 20 per cent drop in their average income).

The growth of exports generally has some favourable social consequences, at least under certain conditions. The increase in export crops by small and medium farmers has a direct favourable effect on the distribution of income and on poverty. In the long term, natural conditions permitting, it leads to the disappearance of subsistence farming, which concerns the poorest families. In doing so, expansion of export crops leads to the progressive disappearance of a reserve of low-productive labour. When this no longer exists, enterprises of the non-agricultural sector must give large wage increases to unskilled workers, which decreases inequality and poverty. If the crops are produced by large farms or plantations, however, increased agricultural exports will not have these favourable social consequences; to the contrary, inequality will become greater and poverty will not decline.

Growth of export industries will also have a favourable impact. Unlike the overprotected industries, they are labour-intensive industries which efficaciously help reduce unemployment. Of course, the wages paid by these industries are low, but they hire workers who previously had still lower incomes, whatever their previous status: unemployed, person active in the informal sector or subsistence farmer. These industries ordinarily pay only the legal minimum wage, if one exists, which means that their employees are at the bottom of the modern sector's income scale. That is why they are often criticised. In many developing countries, however, a majority of the working population has an income less than the legal minimum wage.

In contrast, the growth of mineral exports has, in principle, no positive effect. Mining is highly capital-intensive for technological reasons, it does not provide much employment and its wages are below the average for the modern sector. In fact, the only question involved is the use of surplus mining rent. The appropriation of this rent by the state does not guarantee that it will use this bonus for social purposes — for example, for direct transfers to the poor or investments in rural areas benefiting small peasants — but private appropriation excludes any benefit of this sort. This is not a major issue, however, since structural adjustment measures ordinarily concern only exports of agricultural products and manufactured goods. Mineral exports depend on other, especially exogenous, factors which are ordinarily not affected by adjustment.

In countries having a large public sector, liberalisation is accompanied by privatisation and reform to improve the efficiency of enterprises remaining in the public sector. These decisions entail a number of social consequences; subsidies coming from the taxpayers are abolished; there are wage cuts in those enterprises, which often pay better than the private sector; and rates are raised for electricity, transportation, etc. The most serious consequences obviously are the lay-offs, when there is privatisation or even reorganisation. In countries having a large public sector or when structural adjustment measures involve all enterprises, the cost in unemployment could be very large. Of course, part of the unemployment is absorbed because the unemployed take refuge in the informal sector, but the swelling of its active population automatically reduces average income and increases poverty in cities. For a number of reasons, the growth of exporting industries cannot compensate immediately for these job losses. It takes some time before these enterprises begin to hire, and when they do, they do not recruit workers from the public sector. The state enterprises were noted for their overemployment, most often of men with low productivity resulting from a lack of incentives. Exporting industries like textiles, however, mainly recruit young female workers.

Structural adjustment has some major favourable effects, but an assessment of its social consequences has to take account of the negative effects on employment: the disappearance of semi-clandestine small traders, and lay-offs in overprotected industries and the public sector. These negative effects are greater when there has been exaggerated state control and economic planning before adjustment, as shown by the case of Ghana.

In the medium term, privatisation and other adjustment measures do not compensate the losers. That creates a political and a social problem. Politically, it is obvious that the government of a country like Ghana loses significant support, that of the employees of the public sector, which was the bulk of the modern sector. Of course, to the extent that there is growth of exports of agricultural products and labour-intensive manufactured goods, new groups like peasant exporters, entrepreneurs and workers in export industries will support the government's policy. In the short term, however, there is a problem of political stability: even if the peasants favour the structural adjustment, the government is threatened in cities by the discontent and despair of the tens of thousands of unemployed who have just been laid off. This threat is a political justification for immediate aid to resolve the human problem. In fact, even if the government obtains new supporters among the beneficiaries of its policy, the social problem remains, for these unemployed have no means of subsistence and may remain in that situation even with the development of new economic activity. The gravity of this problem increases with the size of the public sector.

Nonetheless, two favourable effects of structural adjustment should be recalled. First, there is a net social gain from measures which reduce transaction costs and establish free markets. That means they benefit some groups, without loss for any individual. In more technical terms, the economy was functioning below its capacity and the structural adjustment measures bring it closer to the frontier of production. It is certain that poverty is not made worse since there is no loser. Of course, inequality increases if the beneficiaries have incomes higher than the median income, but fiscal measures help redistribute some of the gains. Furthermore, political opposition to these measures should be limited by the fact that no group considers that its interests are hurt, although the weight of custom and tradition may still give rise to opposition.

Furthermore, structural adjustment increases the flexibility of the economy, which is an important social advantage for the future. Exogenous factors may impose a new stabilization programme in several years, but future stabilization measures will be much more efficacious because the economy is more flexible: for example, a revaluation of the exchange rate will lead to a more rapid reallocation of resources between tradable and non-tradable goods. When it becomes easier to make an adjustment, the social costs are less. Thus simulations with the macro-micro model for Morocco show that stabilization causes less unemployment and poverty when the modern sector has flexible prices than when they are rigid.

Now that this portrayal of the effects of structural adjustment is completed, we will see how it can be adapted to minimise social costs. A primary objective should be that the middle- and low-income groups benefit from exports. When export crops come from large plantations, some other steps are necessary. As the agricultural exporting sector is expanding and ordinarily benefits from external loans, these loans could be accorded on condition that new land be reserved for small- and medium-sized farms, which will be given technical assistance so that their output per hectare can reach that of the large plantations. This could increase costs, but the balance of the agricultural exporting sector will shift toward the small and medium farms, which are more labour-intensive. This would involve obvious gains with respect to reducing poverty and increasing social and political stability in rural areas. This policy could be rounded off by imposing a minimum wage on the large plantations that is higher than the equilibrium level in rural areas. This wage could in part be linked to prices of export crops, as is done in Malaysia. This country is of interest because workers on the large rubber plantations have a higher income than small peasants engaged in subsistence farming. In poor or relatively poor countries, wages of certain workers (women, youth) in the export industries are sometimes so low that they do not exceed incomes of subsistence farmers or persons active in the informal sector. Under such conditions, a legal minimum wage above the equilibrium level would be justified because it would not alter the hiring decisions or international competitiveness of these enterprises, while in cities it would have a significant equalising effect on incomes and would reduce poverty. The aptness of such a policy is shown by Morocco, where the government increased the minimum wage in real terms during the adjustment, while average income in the modern sector fell sharply. The minimum wage was no obstacle to rapid growth of exports of manufactured goods or hiring by this sector.

The second problem concerns employment. We have seen that in a case of state socialism (Ghana), structural adjustment to a market economy entailed great costs. The schedule of adjustment is an important variable. It is true that recovery in Ghana occurred first in agricultural exports and then spread to the non-agricultural sector. Thousands of workers are immediately laid off in cities, however, and it takes some years to create jobs. This made it indispensable to have the World Bank-financed compensation programme to aid poor families in cities and help the unemployed establish themselves in their own business or as planters. In a country like Côte d'Ivoire the dimensions of this problem were smaller. Still, there was a grave social problem because the lay-offs in the public sector coincided with the implementation of a stabilization programme, which entailed a drop in activity and employment in the modern private sector. When structural reforms are combined with a stabilization programme, it is always indispensable to have compensatory measures for the effects on employment and poverty in cities. These measures should immediately ensure a vital minimum food ration, like the assistance to women and children described already. On the other hand, they should help the unemployed obtain some capital or skills, so that they can establish themselves in their own business or obtain work in export-oriented sectors, whose growth is promoted by adjustment.

Beyond these compensatory measures, a structural adjustment programme can be rounded off by specific measures to reduce inequalities and poverty. A first example concerns agriculture. Indonesia's experience revealed that investments in rural infrastructure were effective in increasing the productivity and incomes of small peasants who grow rice. Other steps can directly aid food crops to increase the marketable surplus. This agricultural development for the domestic market complements that of export crops, raising low incomes and reducing poverty, while serving to decrease the current account deficit in a country that imports food products. The experience of Latin America during the 1980s shows that the countries able to restore some economic growth were just those having a relatively large and, on the whole, dynamic agricultural sector.

The second example concerns direct taxation. In the difficult context of apportioning the costs of the stabilization programme, public employees and workers in the modern sector are the first affected by measures which appear efficacious and equitable. As these groups resist by all means at their disposal, a political solution might be to link these measures to a reform of direct taxation. In many countries, such a step cannot be implemented at once, given the fiscal system, the fiscal administration's weaknesses, the absence of statistics, etc., but in those rare cases where it is possible, a progressive reform of direct taxation on high incomes could serve as a sort of political compensation to encourage public employees and workers to accept the sacrifices entailed by a stabilization programme.

5. The Role of Donors

It is clear that the IMF and World Bank, as well as bilateral donors, can play a determining role in reducing the costs of adjustment when drawing up the programme. The history of an adjustment is long, extending over a decade. First, this history begins with disequilibria, notably current account and budget deficits which appear two or three years before the financial crisis, since a country should adjust from that moment to reduce the social costs. Then come the crisis, the stabilization programme and, after several months, the structural adjustment programme. The implementation of the last can take several years, and the results of some measures appear only in the medium term, or more than ten years after the first serious disequilibria.

The examples of Indonesia and Malaysia prove that, from a social perspective, it is very desirable for a country to adjust before the crisis. By definition, however, there is little that donors can do to influence a government at this moment, for it can still borrow from foreign banks. It is necessary to increase the donors' means of persuasion. One way would be to offer a country which adjusted before the crisis free insurance against exogenous shocks during adjustment. The high costs of these shocks are well known, whether they result from a deterioration of the terms of trade or a drought or other natural disaster. This insurance could, for example, involve supplying the country with foreign exchange and providing compensatory transfers to the poor in case of a shock. To be a real incentive, this offer should be only valid for a few months. On the other hand, when a country, or group of countries, provides a large amount of aid, it can exercise pressure by offering an adjustment loan at very advantageous terms, the agreement to adjust remaining unofficial. Again this would be temporary offer. In the light of the growing disequilibria, a government would have an incentive to anticipate the crisis and avoid going to the IMF, the gift element of this special aid permitting a reduction in the costs of adjustment, hence making it easier to allocate them. If the government borrows instead of adjusting, it considers the political cost of waiting to be less than the political advantage of not being obliged to allocate the costs of adjustment among the different social groups. The objective of a major donor should be to modify the political costs and advantages which determine a government's choice. An offer of substantial temporary aid to compensate the losses of some groups could change this choice. The international community has another means of persuasion that has virtually no cost — information. A detailed knowledge of the economic situation of each country and all its indebtedness, updated regularly, will deter certain lenders and lead to an earlier outbreak of the financial crisis. Such information would serve as an incentive for a government to accept the offer of special assistance, knowing that the financial crisis is approaching.

If the financial crisis could not be prevented, the donors have two means of reducing the social costs of the stabilization programme and protecting the poor. The first is at the disposition of the IMF when it prepares this programme with the government of the country. As we have seen, other things being equal, it is possible to minimise the costs by adapting the relative weight of the measures. The essential point is that the stabilization measures are not neutral with respect to poverty and income by group, and two programmes providing the same reduction in disequilibria can have different social costs. Thus one objective of a negotiation should be the choice of the programme having the least social costs. This choice has both a technical and a political dimension. It is necessary to have sufficient information and an instrument like the macro-micro model used in our studies, in order to estimate the effects of alternative policies. Several countries should certainly make an effort in this direction. When it is impossible to produce and collect the necessary statistics, priority can be given to stabilization measures which have proved the most satisfactory for other countries at a similar level of development. As to the political aspects, it is a matter of disarming the influential groups in opposition, for often the socially optimal programme is not politically feasible. The IMF has two arguments: the first is that an IMF loan is indispensable to a country in crisis, the second is to call on bilateral donors for the compensatory transfers.

Thus we reach the complementary role of donors. They can finance two types of transfers. Some prevent any augmentation of poverty, for even an optimal programme often involves some increase in poverty. The second ensures the political feasibility of the programme by benefiting some of the groups opposing it. This involves providing them with some compensation to cushion the unfavourable impact of the programme on their living standards. Often the two types of transfers are merged: the same aid is used for the poor and for other groups especially affected by the stabilization programme. An example would be free meals in primary and secondary schools. Foreign aid could finance these meals in poor districts as a compensation for income losses of poor families, but this measure could be extended to all schools: if public employees and modern sector workers bear the principal cost of the stabilization measures, their opposition will be attenuated by these free meals. Moreover, they profit much more than poor households from meals in secondary schools. Thus the donor can consider this transfer as devoted partly to fighting an increase in poverty and partly to ensuring the stabilization programme is politically feasible.

Foreign assistance appears to be essential for financing these compensatory measures in view of their cost at a time of budget deficit. In Morocco, the transfers needed to compensate the growth of poverty represented 5 per cent of public expenditures. In Ecuador, they were even higher since they reached 3.5 per cent of GDP. Owing to the budget deficit and drastic cuts imposed by the stabilization programme, it was impossible for the state to finance them. Resorting to money creation has obvious drawbacks in an economy under inflationary pressure. The advantage of targeted external financing is that its opportunity cost is zero; the funds are available only, for example, for school meals. If these transfers take the form of gifts, they have no impact on the debt. Thus they ensure that the stabilization programme is politically feasible, prevent an increase in poverty and have no effect on reducing disequilibria and debt. (The only possible drawback would be a price increase if demand centres on non-tradable goods, which is rare; but if it is a question of tradable goods, the transfers finance supplementary imports.) If the donor participates in the negotiations on the stabilization programme, this gives the IMF a means of pressure to obtain acceptance of the socially optimal programme, for if the groups affected by the stabilization programme reject it, they lose the advantages provided by the donor. Some parties may criticise the offer of grants instead of loans, but there is good justification for the former. First, it makes no sense to increase the debt for social reasons in a financial crisis; second, it is easier to control the use of a grant. In the hypothetical case above, for example, a donor financing all school canteens could demand the right to supervise them directly. Finally, this is a temporary charge, since the aid is granted only for the duration of the stabilization programme, for two or three years if it succeeds. Improved statistical information would enable donors to target grants better, but they could act even when there is insufficient information, since an extension of the transfers to other groups may be politically necessary.

This subject is also related to the widely discussed problem of conditionality of aid. Donors cannot afford to make these grants if they are not sure that the beneficiary country is doing what is necessary to minimise the social costs of adjustment. A determination to do this may be lacking, for the poor, especially the rural poor, ordinarily do not have much political strength. Thus it is desirable that international organisations and donors clearly make the objective of equity a condition of loans and grants, whether it is a question of drawing up a stabilization programme or implementing compensatory measures.

The donors' role in devising and implementing structural adjustment programmes is different, since these measures act in the medium and long term, and sometimes are not specific to adjustment. The latter is true in the aforementioned examples of investments in rural areas and reform of income taxes. Social considerations could easily justify loans and/or technical assistance, but the World Bank and donors could support the same policy in an economy in which macroeconomic disequilibria are absent.

On the other hand, structural adjustment raises two distinctive problems, of which the first is reorienting an economy towards foreign markets. This orientation often has favourable effects on the distribution of income and on poverty, but not always, as has been seen. It is necessary to take this into account in loans for financing new export activities, so that the latter will have favourable repercussions for the middle- and low-income groups. When export crops are the monopoly of big farms or plantations, loans for extending these crops should be conditioned on a change in agrarian patterns: establishment of small and medium farms on the new land, even a gradual redistribution of some of the land already cultivated. This policy does not exclude large plantations, which can play a positive role in the technical domain, but its objective is to create a large group of small- and medium-sized exporting planters, because the reduction of inequality and poverty in rural areas depends on the emergence of such a group.

The second problem is the urban unemployment and poverty caused by the combination of privatisations, reforms and lay-offs in the state enterprises, together with a relative liberalisation of manufactured imports and the stabilization measures. Depending on the country, these can be more or less grave, extremely serious in a country like Ghana, negligible in other cases, as in Malaysia. When all the adjustment measures are implemented at the same time there is danger of creating an explosive situation in urban areas, which makes external aid imperative. Even if all the donors (international organisations and countries) work together, this involves a very large expenditure, much larger than the cost of compensatory transfers to prevent an increase in poverty during stabilization (see above). In fact, it is necessary to finance a sort of social safety net for the urban population during the more or less long period of structural transition. Of course, this cost can partly be financed by loans. For example, grants can cover such things as a guaranteed minimum food ration, but loans be used for productive capital or retraining of the unemployed since these will increase a country's production and thus its repayment capabilities. In other respects, it might be thought that staggering the reforms of the public sector would spread out the social costs, but this solution, based on financial considerations, could be a political error. In maintaining a large public sector, it leaves intact the influence of a powerful pressure group (workers and managers of these enterprises), implacably hostile to all structural adjustment. In countries where the majority of the population derives its living from agriculture, a rapid conversion is much less costly because the urban public sector is much less important than in the countries of Eastern Europe. When grants permit compensation for the social costs, as in Ghana, perhaps this shock treatment is the best solution. Of course, the donors are not historically responsible for the problem, but by preventing an increase in urban poverty during the transition period, they provide these countries with the ability to continue their development by their own means. Thus by accepting a heavier burden today, the donors free themselves from a future responsibility.

Note

1. Cf. Nelson (1989) and Nelson (1990).

Bibliography

I. Development Centre Country Studies

DEMERY, D. and L. DEMERY (1991), *Adjustment and Equity in Malaysia.*

DE JANVRY, A., E. SADOULET and A. FARGEIX (1991), *Adjustment and Equity in Ecuador.*

MELLER, P. (1991), *Adjustment and Equity in Chile.*

MORRISSON, C. (1991), *Adjustment and Equity in Morocco.*

ROE, A. and H. SCHNEIDER (1992), *Adjustment and Equity in Ghana.*

SCHNEIDER, H. (1991), *Adjustment and Equity in Côte d'Ivoire.*

THORBECKE, E. (1991), *Adjustment and Equity in Indonesia.*

II. Books and Articles

ADDISON, T., L. DEMERY, J. ROUND, T. STEPHENS and M. FERRONI (1990), *Adjustment and Poverty: A Conceptual, Empirical and Policy Framework*, World Bank, Washington.

ADELMAN, I. and S. ROBINSON (1978), *Income Distribution Policy in Developing Countries: A Case Study of Korea*, Stanford University Press, Stanford.

AZAM, J.P., C. CHAMBAS and P. and S. GUILLAUMONT (1989), *The Impact of Macroeconomic Policies for the Rural Poor*, UNDP, Policy Discussion Paper, New York.

BARRO, R. and X. SALA I. MARTIN (1990), "Public Finance in Models of Economic Growth", *NBER*, No. 3362, New York.

BLEJER, M. and I. GUERRERO (1990), "The Impact of Macroeconomic Policies on Income Distribution: An Empirical Study of the Philippines", *Review of Economics and Statistics.*

BOURGUIGNON, F., J. DE MELO and C. MORRISSON (1991), "Adjustment with Growth and Equity: A Symposium", *World Development.*

BOURGUIGNON, F., W. BRANSON and J. DE MELO (1989), *Macroeconomic Adjustment and Income Distribution: A Macro-Micro Simulation Model*, OECD Development Centre Technical Paper No. 1, Paris.

BOURGUIGNON, F., W. BRANSON and J. DE MELO (1992), "Adjustment and Income Distribution: A Micro-Macro Model for Counterfactual Analysis", *Journal of Development Economics.*

BOURGUIGNON, F. and C. MORRISSON (1989), *External Trade and Income Distribution*, OECD Development Centre, Paris.

BOURGUIGNON, F., J. DE MELO and A. SUWA (1991), "Distributional Effects of Adjustment Policies: Simulation for Two Archetype Economics in Africa and Latin America", *World Bank Economic Review*.

BRANSON, W. (1989) *Macroeconomic Theory and Policy*, Harper and Row, New York.

CORNIA, A., R. JOLLY and F. STEWART (1987), *Adjustment With a Human Face*, UNICEF, New York.

DERVIS, K., J. DE MELO and S. ROBINSON (1982), *General Equilibrium Models for Development Policy*, Cambridge University Press, Cambridge.

JOHNSON, O. and J. SALOP (1980), "Distributional Aspects of Stabilization Programs in Developing Countries", IMF, Staff Papers, Washington.

HELLER, P., A. BOVENBERG, T. CATSAMBAS, KE-YOUNG CHU and P. SHOME (1988), *The Implications of Fund-Supported Adjustment Programs for Poverty. Experiences in Selected Countries*, IMF, Washington.

HOOD, R., J. MCGUIRE and M. STARR (1988), "The Socioeconomic Impact of Macroeconomic Adjustment", Center for Development Technology, International Science and Technology Institute, mimeo, Washington.

KANBUR, R. (1987), "Measurement and Alleviation of Poverty: with an Application to the Effects of Macroeconomic Adjustment", IMF, Staff Papers, Washington.

KANBUR, R. (1987), "Structural Adjustment, Macroeconomic Adjustment and Poverty: A Methodology for Analysis", *World Development*.

MAASLAND, A. (1990), *Methods for Measuring the Effect of Adjustment Politics on Income Distribution*, World Bank, W.P.S. 474, Washington.

N'CHO-OGUIE, C. (1989), *Integrating Social Dimensions in Macroeconomic Adjustment Policy Analysis: Towards a Modelling Strategy*, University of San Francisco, San Francisco.

NELSON, J. (ed). (1989), *Fragile Coalitions: The Politics of Economic Adjustment*, Transaction, New Brunswick.

NELSON, J. (ed). (1990), *Economic Crisis and Policy Choice. The Politics of Adjustment in the Third World*, Princeton University Press, Princeton.

PFEFFERMAN, G. (1986), *Poverty in Latin America: The Impact of Depression*, World Bank, Washington.

ROLAND-HOLST, D. (1992), "Stabilization and Structural Adjustment in Indonesia: an Intertemporal General Equilibrium Analysis", mimeo, OECD Development Centre, Paris.

SCOBIE, G. (1989), *Macroeconomic Adjustment and the Poor: Towards a Research Strategy*, Cornell University, Ithaca.

TAYLOR, L. (1990), *The Varieties of Stabilization Experiences*, Oxford University Press, Oxford.

TAYLOR, L. and F. LISY (1979), "Vanishing Income Redistribution: Keynesian Clues About Model Surprises in the Short Run", *Journal of Development Economics*.

TOBIN, J. (1969), "A General Equilibrium Approach to Monetary Theory", *Journal of Money, Credit and Banking*.

WORLD BANK (1990), *Analysis Plans for Understanding the Social Dimensions of Adjustment*, Washington.

WORLD BANK and UNDP (1989), *The Social Dimensions of Structural Adjustment in Sub-Saharan Africa* - (3 volumes), Washington.

WORLD BANK (1990), "Poverty and Adjustment. A Literature Review", mimeo, Economic Development Institute, Washington.

WORLD BANK (1989 and 1990), *Adjustment Lending Report PPR*, Washington.

MAIN SALES OUTLETS OF OECD PUBLICATIONS – PRINCIPAUX POINTS DE VENTE DES PUBLICATIONS DE L'OCDE

Argentina – Argentine
Carlos Hirsch S.R.L.
Galería Güemes, Florida 165, 4° Piso
1333 Buenos Aires   Tel. (1) 331.1787 y 331.2391
                                          Telefax: (1) 331.1787

Australia – Australie
D.A. Book (Aust.) Pty. Ltd.
648 Whitehorse Road, P.O.B 163
Mitcham, Victoria 3132   Tel. (03) 873.4411
                                          Telefax: (03) 873.5679

Austria – Autriche
OECD Publications and Information Centre
Schedestrasse 7
D-W 5300 Bonn 1 (Germany)   Tel. (49.228) 21.60.45
                                          Telefax: (49.228) 26.11.04

Gerold & Co.
Graben 31
Wien I   Tel. (0222) 533.50.14

Belgium – Belgique
Jean De Lannoy
Avenue du Roi 202
B-1060 Bruxelles   Tel. (02) 538.51.69/538.08.41
                                          Telefax: (02) 538.08.41

Canada
Renouf Publishing Company Ltd.
1294 Algoma Road
Ottawa, ON K1B 3W8   Tel. (613) 741.4333
                                          Telefax: (613) 741.5439
Stores:
61 Sparks Street
Ottawa, ON K1P 5R1   Tel. (613) 238.8985
211 Yonge Street
Toronto, ON M5B 1M4   Tel. (416) 363.3171
Federal Publications
165 University Avenue
Toronto, ON M5H 3B8   Tel. (416) 581.1552
                                          Telefax: (416)581.1743
Les Éditions La Liberté Inc.
3020 Chemin Sainte-Foy
Sainte-Foy, PQ G1X 3V6   Tel. (418) 658.3763
                                          Telefax: (418) 658.3763

China – Chine
China National Publications Import
   Export Corporation (CNPIEC)
P.O. Box 88
Beijing   Tel. 44.0731
                                          Telefax: 401.5661

Denmark – Danemark
Munksgaard Export and Subscription Service
35, Nørre Søgade, P.O. Box 2148
DK-1016 København K   Tel. (33) 12.85.70
                                          Telefax: (33) 12.93.87

Finland – Finlande
Akateeminen Kirjakauppa
Keskuskatu 1, P.O. Box 128
00100 Helsinki   Tel. (358 0) 12141
                                          Telefax: (358 0) 121.4441

France
OECD/OCDE
Mail Orders/Commandes par correspondance:
2, rue André-Pascal
75775 Paris Cédex 16   Tel. (33-1) 45.24.82.00
                                       Telefax: (33-1) 45.24.85.00
                                          or (33-1) 45.24.81.76
                                          Telex: 620 160 OCDE

Bookshop/Librairie:
33, rue Octave-Feuillet
75016 Paris   Tel. (33-1) 45.24.81.67
                                             (33-1) 45.24.81.81

Librairie de l'Université
12a, rue Nazareth
13100 Aix-en-Provence   Tel. 42.26.18.08
                                          Telefax: 42.26.63.26

Germany – Allemagne
OECD Publications and Information Centre
Schedestrasse 7
D-W 5300 Bonn 1   Tel. (0228) 21.60.45
                                          Telefax: (0228) 26.11.04

Greece – Grèce
Librairie Kauffmann
Mavrokordatou 9
106 78 Athens   Tel. 322.21.60
                                          Telefax: 363.39.67

Hong Kong
Swindon Book Co. Ltd.
13 - 15 Lock Road
Kowloon, Hong Kong   Tel. 366.80.31
                                          Telefax: 739.49.75

Iceland – Islande
Mál Mog Menning
Laugavegi 18, Pósthólf 392
121 Reykjavik   Tel. 162.35.23

India – Inde
Oxford Book and Stationery Co.
Scindia House
New Delhi 110001   Tel.(11) 331.5896/5308
                                          Telefax: (11) 332.5993
17 Park Street
Calcutta 700016   Tel. 240832

Indonesia – Indonésie
Pdii-Lipi
P.O. Box 269/JKSMG/88
Jakarta 12790   Tel. 583467
                                          Telex: 62 875

Ireland – Irlande
TDC Publishers – Library Suppliers
12 North Frederick Street
Dublin 1   Tel. 74.48.35/74.96.77
                                          Telefax: 74.84.16

Israel
Electronic Publications only
Publications électroniques seulement
Sophist Systems Ltd.
71 Allenby Street
Tel-Aviv 65134   Tel. 3-29.00.21
                                          Telefax: 3-29.92.39

Italy – Italie
Libreria Commissionaria Sansoni
Via Duca di Calabria 1/1
50125 Firenze   Tel. (055) 64.54.15
                                          Telefax: (055) 64.12.57
Via Bartolini 29
20155 Milano   Tel. (02) 36.50.83
Editrice e Libreria Herder
Piazza Montecitorio 120
00186 Roma   Tel. 679.46.28
                                          Telex: NATEL I 621427
Libreria Hoepli
Via Hoepli 5
20121 Milano   Tel. (02) 86.54.46
                                          Telefax: (02) 805.28.86
Libreria Scientifica
Dott. Lucio de Biasio 'Aeiou'
Via Meravigli 16
20123 Milano   Tel. (02) 805.68.98
                                          Telefax: (02) 80.01.75

Japan – Japon
OECD Publications and Information Centre
Landic Akasaka Building
2-3-4 Akasaka, Minato-ku
Tokyo 107   Tel. (81.3) 3586.2016
                                          Telefax: (81.3) 3584.7929

Korea – Corée
Kyobo Book Centre Co. Ltd.
P.O. Box 1658, Kwang Hwa Moon
Seoul   Tel. 730.78.91
                                          Telefax: 735.00.30

Malaysia – Malaisie
Co-operative Bookshop Ltd.
University of Malaya
P.O. Box 1127, Jalan Pantai Baru
59700 Kuala Lumpur
Malaysia   Tel. 756.5000/756.5425
                                          Telefax: 757.3661

Netherlands – Pays-Bas
SDU Uitgeverij
Christoffel Plantijnstraat 2
Postbus 20014
2500 EA's-Gravenhage   Tel. (070 3) 78.99.11
Voor bestellingen: Tel. (070 3) 78.98.80
                                          Telefax: (070 3) 47.63.51

New Zealand – Nouvelle-Zélande
GP Publications Ltd.
Customer Services
33 The Esplanade - P.O. Box 38-900
Petone, Wellington   Tel. (04) 5685.555
                                          Telefax: (04) 5685.333

Norway – Norvège
Narvesen Info Center - NIC
Bertrand Narvesens vei 2
P.O. Box 6125 Etterstad
0602 Oslo 6   Tel. (02) 57.33.00
                                          Telefax: (02) 68.19.01

Pakistan
Mirza Book Agency
65 Shahrah Quaid-E-Azam
Lahore 3   Tel. 66.839
                                  Telex: 44886 UBL PK. Attn: MIRZA BK

Portugal
Livraria Portugal
Rua do Carmo 70-74
Apart. 2681
1117 Lisboa Codex   Tel.: (01) 347.49.82/3/4/5
                                          Telefax: (01) 347.02.64

Singapore – Singapour
Information Publications Pte. Ltd.
Pei-Fu Industrial Building
24 New Industrial Road No. 02-06
Singapore 1953   Tel. 283.1786/283.1798
                                          Telefax: 284.8875

Spain – Espagne
Mundi-Prensa Libros S.A.
Castelló 37, Apartado 1223
Madrid 28001   Tel. (91) 431.33.99
                                          Telefax: (91) 575.39.98
Libreria Internacional AEDOS
Consejo de Ciento 391
08009 - Barcelona   Tel. (93) 488.34.92
                                          Telefax: (93) 487.76.59
Llibreria de la Generalitat
Palau Moja
Rambla dels Estudis, 118
08002 - Barcelona   Tel. (93) 318.80.12 (Subscripcions)
                                (93) 302.67.23 (Publicacions)
                                          Telefax: (93) 412.18.54

Sri Lanka
Centre for Policy Research
c/o Colombo Agencies Ltd.
No. 300-304, Galle Road
Colombo 3   Tel. (1) 574240, 573551-2
                                          Telefax: (1) 575394, 510711

Sweden – Suède
Fritzes Fackboksföretaget
Box 16356
Regeringsgatan 12
103 27 Stockholm   Tel. (08) 23.89.00
                                          Telefax: (08) 20.50.21
Subscription Agency/Abonnements:
Wennergren-Williams AB
Nordenflychtsvägen 74
Box 30004
104 25 Stockholm   Tel. (08) 13.67.00
                                          Telefax: (08) 618.62.32

Switzerland – Suisse
OECD Publications and Information Centre
Schedestrasse 7
D-W 5300 Bonn 1 (Germany)   Tel. (49.228) 21.60.45
                                          Telefax: (49.228) 26.11.04

Suisse romande
Maditec S.A.
Chemin des Palettes 4
1020 Renens/Lausanne   Tel. (021) 635.08.65
                                          Telefax: (021) 635.07.80
Librairie Payot
6 rue Grenus
1211 Genève 11   Tel. (022) 731.89.50
                                          Telex: 28356
Subscription Agency – Service des Abonnements
Naville S.A.
7, rue Lévrier
1201 Genève   Tél.: (022) 732.24.00
                                          Telefax: (022) 738.87.13

Taiwan – Formose
Good Faith Worldwide Int'l. Co. Ltd.
9th Floor, No. 118, Sec. 2
Chung Hsiao E. Road
Taipei   Tel. (02) 391.7396/391.7397
                                          Telefax: (02) 394.9176

Thailand – Thaïlande
Suksit Siam Co. Ltd.
113, 115 Fuang Nakhon Rd.
Opp. Wat Rajbopith
Bangkok 10200   Tel. (662) 251.1630
                                          Telefax: (662) 236.7783

Turkey – Turquie
Kültur Yayinlari Is-Türk Ltd. Sti.
Atatürk Bulvari No. 191/Kat. 21
Kavaklidere/Ankara   Tel. 25.07.60
Dolmabahce Cad. No. 29
Besiktas/Istanbul   Tel. 160.71.88
                                          Telex: 43482B

United Kingdom – Royaume-Uni
HMSO
Gen. enquiries   Tel. (071) 873 0011
Postal orders only:
P.O. Box 276, London SW8 5DT
Personal Callers HMSO Bookshop
49 High Holborn, London WC1V 6HB
                                          Telefax: 071 873 2000
         Branches at: Belfast, Birmingham, Bristol, Edinburgh,
                                                                   Manchester

United States – États-Unis
OECD Publications and Information Centre
2001 L Street N.W., Suite 700
Washington, D.C. 20036-4910   Tel. (202) 785.6323
                                          Telefax: (202) 785.0350

Venezuela
Libreria del Este
Avda F. Miranda 52, Aptdo. 60337
Edificio Galipán
Caracas 106   Tel. 951.1705/951.2307/951.1297
                                          Telegram: Libreste Caracas

Yugoslavia – Yougoslavie
Jugoslovenska Knjiga
Knez Mihajlova 2, P.O. Box 36
Beograd   Tel. (011) 621.992
                                          Telefax: (011) 625.970

Orders and inquiries from countries where Distributors have
not yet been appointed should be sent to: OECD Publications Service, 2 rue André-Pascal, 75775 Paris Cédex 16,
France.

Les commandes provenant de pays où l'OCDE n'a pas
encore désigné de distributeur devraient être adressées à :
OCDE, Service des Publications, 2, rue André-Pascal, 75775
Paris Cédex 16, France.

OECD PUBLICATIONS, 2 rue André-Pascal, 75775 PARIS CEDEX 16
PRINTED IN FRANCE
(41 91 22 1) ISBN 92-64-13664-9 - No. 46087 1992